Ripper
Killers

First published in 2014

A catalogue record for this book is available from the British Library

ISBN: 978-0-85733-668-2

Published by Haynes Publishing, Sparkford, Yeovil,
Somerset BA22 7JJ, UK
Tel: 01963 442030 Fax: 01963 440001
Int. tel: +44 1963 442030 Int. fax: +44 1963 440001
E-mail: sales@haynes.co.uk
Website: www.haynes.co.uk

Haynes North America Inc., 861 Lawrence Drive, Newbury Park, California 91320, USA

Images © Mirrorpix

Creative Director: Kevin Gardner
Designed for Haynes by BrainWave

Printed and bound in the US

From The Case Files of

Claire Welch

Contents

Introduction

Ripper killers have been feared the world over since the heinous crimes of Jack the Ripper in Whitechapel, London, in the late 19th century. As an unidentified perpetrator of the mutilation and murder of his victims, "Jack" as he was dubbed, wasn't the first serial killer in history, but the horrors of the case soon whipped up a media frenzy, the like of which had never been seen before.

Ripper killers generally share similar traits or have the same type of *modus operandi* (MO), where the use of knives and mutilation of victims, often women, are commonplace. Knives are easier to get hold of than many other types of weapon, and provide the ripper killer with the perfect tool with which to vent his extreme rage and anger at his vulnerable victims, who often suffer extreme torture at their hands before they face an inevitable death. Victims are often subjected to being violently ripped open by their killer and many are dismembered.

Most, but not all, ripper killers target prostitutes. The fact that these women work on the fringes of society makes them extremely vulnerable to attack. "Jack the Ripper" was infamous for the mutilation and disembowelling of his victims. Peter Sutcliffe, the Yorkshire Ripper, mutilated and bit his victims, and it was these bite marks that would lead to his eventual arrest, although years later experts could not agree that the bite marks actually came from the murderer in the case of Josephine Whitaker. The Gainsville Ripper, Danny Rolling, also mutilated his victims, and posed them, sometimes using mirrors, so that the impact when their bodies were discovered would be heightened. Like Jack the Ripper, the Craigslist Ripper has never been caught, while perhaps the worst of them all was Andrei Chikatilo, the Soviet serial killer dubbed the Rostov Ripper. Chikatilo was responsible for the deaths of at least 53 victims, many of them children, who were mutilated by his teeth, knives and sticks before being strangled and battered.

By 2nd January 1981, with the Yorkshire Ripper still on the loose, and rape statistics soaring, police took a major step to prevent women from defending themselves with a comparatively harmless device. What police didn't know at the time the papers reported that a London woman, Caroline Farnejad, was given an unbelievable one-month suspended jail sentence for carrying a harmless spray in her handbag, was that Yorkshire police would apprehend Peter Sutcliffe that very same day.

The spray, sold and used legally in the United States, contained pepper juice, and marked an attacker in the face with red dye. Police, however, classified it as a firearm. A Scotland Yard spokesman spelled out the law as it stood and said: "We cannot recommend women to carry anything in their handbags which might be constituted as an offensive weapon." The only item that women could use legally was a screaming device – which women's groups had tried out and declared useless. Sheila Joy, of Women Against Violence said: "What chance does a woman have to protect herself if she is about to be assaulted? She is physically weaker than a man and if she carries anything to protect herself she is discriminated against." MP Gwilym

Roberts was to write to the then Home Secretary, Willie Whitelaw, asking for the 1968 Firearms Act to be amended. "As the law stands at the moment virtually anything a woman carries in her handbag could be classified as an offensive weapon if used during an attack. What we need to define is the purpose for which an object is being carried," he said. The police advice at the time, being distributed in the Ripper country of South Yorkshire, simply urged women not to walk alone at night, to keep away from unlit areas, and to scream loudly if attacked. Carrying the harmless spray was likely to land a woman in court.

Two years later, in July 1983, Britain's first serious attempt to programme a computer to catch a killer began. Four leading police officers and a Home Office computer expert met to lay down guidelines for the inquiry into the deaths of five-year-old Caroline Hogg and Susan Maxwell, aged 11, prior to the capture, arrest and successful conviction of Robert Black. The bodies of Caroline, from Edinburgh, and Susan, from Northumberland, were found just 30 miles apart in the Midlands. At the meeting, held in Edinburgh, where a £1.8 million police computer was destined to be used in the programme, were Assistant Chief Constable Hector Clerk, of Northumbria, and senior detectives from Edinburgh, Leicester and Stafford, along with the computer expert. The computer was expected to do in seconds what had previously been a laborious, endless cross-checking of statements, and car movements that had taken many, many human hours to complete. It was partly the failure of the police's "hand-operated" checking system that had allowed the Yorkshire Ripper to evade arrest for so long.

In 1994, the *Mirror* reported: "Charles Manson, Jeffrey Dahmer, David Berkowitz ... they shocked the world with the depths of their evil, yet now the world is cashing in." The article, published in April that year described how public fascination with the worst murders in history had reached an all-time high, as had the temptation to make a "killing" from the men whose vicious crimes had turned them in to twisted cult heroes. Shockingly, the market for cards, posters and songs was prolific. It seemed that nothing was taboo as long as it made money. Even the killers themselves were seizing the chance to rake in the dollars. Jeffrey Dahmer, the cannibal killer of Milwaukee who butchered 17 young men and ate parts of their bodies was, by the early 1990s, trying to auction off his grisly assortment of personal possessions, including the fridge where police discovered human hamburgers made from his victims. Far from being shunned, he was deluged with love letters and cash. At least £6,000 was sent to him by one woman in Chelsea, London. The paper went on to report how, for the equivalent of £1.60, anyone in the United States could dial a dedicated telephone number and be connected to the recorded voice of John Wayne Gacy, who made his name as the biggest mass murderer on death row, where he awaited execution for his sex killings of 33 young men. Bizarrely, in between bouts of bloodletting, Gacy used to dress as Pogo the Clown to entertain neighbourhood kids in Chicago. (Gacy was a huge charity fundraiser prior to his capture and convictions.) However, while waiting to die, Gacy's telephone message was a massive money-spinner. His paintings of clowns, done as he awaited his fate, fetched upwards of £15,000 each and were exhibited in swanky galleries from Los Angeles to Texas. Meanwhile, posters of Dahmer were snapped up by "fans", as were those of David Koresh, the cult leader who died in the infamous Waco siege in Texas. Charles Manson didn't miss out either. Axl Rose recorded a song about the man whose evil "family" massacred seven people, including the pregnant actress Sharon Tate, in 1969. Another serial killer to find himself on the end of money-making schemes was Joel Rifkin, who went on trial in Long Island in May 1994 after a three-year killing spree during which he murdered 17 prostitutes. Traffic police in the US apprehended Rifkin as he shone a torch light on his final dead victim, bound in the boot of his car. "We Love Joel" newsletters were already being circulated before the killer went on trial. Like Gacy and Dahmer, Rifkin was swamped with "fan" letters in his cell. What the *Mirror* particularly objected to was the startling yardstick of America's moral decline through the "adulation of these beasts ... [in] serial killer trading cards collections...issued with bubble gum."

"Worship of these monsters", stated the *Mirror*, "appalls William Birnes, co-author of a book, *Serial Killers*." Birnes said: "Society's fascination may not create these people, but it certainly encourages them." And, perhaps the most celebrated of them all is Jack the Ripper, who, despite never being named, is the subject of countless books, journals, articles and films, and is the inspiration for many TV series and documentaries. Whatever the fascination that turns these killers into "cult" figures, is the subject of much debate, but one thing is pretty clear, even into the 21st century, the obsession with murderers, and ripper killers in particular, isn't on the wane.

By the start of the 21st century, the police had a new weapon to deploy in the pursuit of rapists and murderers. She looked like an attractive businesswoman with immaculate blonde hair, perfect nails and elegant suit, but Helen Skelton's profession would leave most people quivering. As a psychological profiler, a female "Cracker", it was Helen's mission in the early 2000s to get into the minds of Britain's most evil rapists – and put them behind bars. Softly spoken, Skelton, headed a team of analysts at the National Crime Squad, the elite intelligence-gathering organization often compared with the Federal Bureau of Investigation (FBI) in the United States. She was the only female boss in the service and it was her job, every day, to deal with cases and sights that would have seen even hardened professionals recoil in horror. Helen had already put away Michael Sams, kidnapper of estate agent Stephanie Slater, and cold-blooded killer of prostitute Julie Dart, in one of the most notorious cases at the end of the 20th century. Despite her high-profile career, she told the *Mirror* that she would never get over the cruelty that men and women inflict upon each other. "Those emotions don't go away, but I have learnt to hide them ... When you spend a lot of time looking at sexual violence, child abuse and murder, you see some of the cruellest aspects of life. I studied investigative psychology to learn how one human being can do something like that to another and still carry on." Having obtained her masters degree, Helen went on to specialize in researching the motivations of sex offenders. Her essential role was to collect information from contacts, witnesses and police surveillance before putting it together, using charts to plot the movements and characteristics of the suspect. In cases where rape turned into murder, the job entailed filling in as many gaps as possible, including who the victim associated with, and what happened immediately before and after the crime. Analysis of all this information would often lead to new leads. Helen conducted extensive research into the psychology of rapists and compared the circumstances of date rape, referred to as non-stranger rape, with rape by an unknown man. At the time of the *Mirror*'s article in 2000, rape was still a very under-reported crime, although a high percentage of rapists had convictions for other crimes. At the turn of the 21st century around 40 per cent of those who knew their victims were serial rapists. Today, in the United States, it is reported that 73 per cent of rapes are committed by a non-stranger and more than four in 10 rapes take place at the victim's home. Of the 73 per cent, 38 per cent of rapists are a friend or acquaintance, 28 per cent are an intimate partner, or from an intimate relationship, and seven per cent are related to their victim according to the Rape, Abuse and Incest National Network. In the UK, shockingly low figures were recorded for convictions of known rapists at the beginning of 2013. Around 95,000 women are raped in the UK each year, but just over 1,000 men are convicted. Men who are victims of rape are even less likely to see their perpetrator brought to justice. It is estimated that by the time we reach the start of the third decade of the new millennium, around 90 per cent of rape victims in the UK will know the identity of their attacker.

The long-thought stereotype of a man in a balaclava hiding behind a bush waiting for a victim is rarely the reality – although with ripper killers random victims are picked. Rapists progress quickly. While they may wine and dine their first few victims, by the time the attacker has reached up to 10 rapes, the victim may have been picked up at a club and lured to a car where they're beaten before being raped. This can escalate particularly quickly. When crimes of this nature are committed, psychological profilers have to work out what sort of person is behind the attack and try to pre-empt their next move. They work around the clock looking at forensic evidence and the movements of the victim. It is also the job of a profiler to work with sex offenders and other criminals to understand their motivations and to devise effective treatments in order to prevent reoffending. Over the past decade, techniques and technologies have become more sophisticated, and those working with violent criminals are increasingly optimistic that more perpetrators will be stopped.

Unfortunately, sex workers are more vulnerable to violent attacks than many other people in society. "It is the world's oldest profession and according to many", reported the *Mirror* in 2003, "the laws surrounding prostitution in Britain have been stuck in time too." After centuries of conflict between sex workers, government, police and pressure groups, there was some hope of common ground – that of change. Early in the 2000s there were calls to legalize prostitution, and to set up special "zones", where people could openly buy sex.

Those in favour hoped it would become a reality by 2013. At the time of writing, the debate rages on. But back in 2003, even the Metropolitan Police Commander, Andrew Baker, added his voice to the campaign. He told a conference in Birmingham that the UK could learn a lot from countries such as Holland, where special zones were in operation. In the wake of the Camden Ripper case – which saw three London prostitutes murdered by their client – Anthony Hardy, the head of Scotland Yard's homicide squad argued for tighter rules to keep sex workers safe. "There is a need now for an informed debate," he said. "We know that sex workers are vulnerable. I know that attacks, violence, drugs and criminal control are lower in tolerance zones." At the beginning of the 21st century, sex workers generated around £700 million a year in Britain. The need to ensure that these workers were less vulnerable than they had been for thousands of years was paramount – and still is. In 2002, 150 workers were accepted as union members for the first time in an offshoot of the general trade union, the GMB, which marked a huge step towards tighter regulation of the traditionally underground industry. The union then added its support to the campaign for legislation. At the time, there were 36 types of legislation relating to prostitution, many of which were contradictory or nonsensical. Today, there are many different kinds of sexual violence, which includes (but is certainly not restricted to) rape, sexual assault, child sexual abuse, sexual harassment, rape within marriage or relationships, forced marriage, so-called honour-based violence, female genital mutilation, trafficking, sexual exploitation, and ritual abuse, alongside digital rape.

Special zones for those working in the sex industry still seem aeons away. Those living near to proposed areas don't want the business outside their front doors, or in a house or flat on their street, but distancing workers by isolating them far from residential areas just puts them at greater risk. Those against the special zones believe that they will be a magnet for other criminal activities and sex offenders. For now, this is still a legal and moral minefield.

There is no perfect crime. Every murder has a trail that can be followed back, no matter how cunning the killer, hoped the police towards the end of 2006. At the time they were hunting the man responsible for the murder of at least three prostitutes in Ipswich. However, unlike TV series such as *Cracker, CSI, Body of Proof* and *Waking the Dead*, where a carefully followed trail leads directly to the killer, real-life investigations, such as the Green River Killer, who murdered 48 sex workers in Seattle, are fiendishly difficult to solve. The reason, say police, is simple. In serial killing, and ripper killings, the only relationship between the victim and the killer is the act of murder itself. The *Mirror* reported in 2006: "The killer and victim meet, drive off together and 30 minutes later the victim could be dead and dumped." It is chilling to think this happens much more often than people realize. The killer could be any adult male. The time, date and scene of crime, and the killer's car are all unknown. All that remains, said the newspaper: "is the naked body of his victim, killed somewhere then dumped in water to destroy all DNA evidence."

The Ipswich murder team were well aware that the murderer would continue to kill unless he was caught. Their killer, however, was leaving vital clues. The man was obviously local and knew how to dispose of his victims' bodies without being disturbed – he had an intimate local knowledge of the area, which pointed to the possibility that his hobbies included fishing or walking. Police were able to use the profiles of the Yorkshire Ripper to help them track down the Ipswich serial killer. As far back as the late 1970s, Peter Sutcliffe was nearly caught by police cameras logging number plates of punters cruising red-light districts in Leeds and Bradford, but a blunder helped him slip through the net. In Ipswich, with its town centre ringed with CCTV cameras, the police knew that somewhere, at some point, the killer's car must have been clocked.

Police now follow well-established patterns first discovered by the FBI, where serial killers, and ripper killers, are highly likely to have minor convictions for kerb-crawling or public indecency. In serial killers, the removal of the victim's clothes may be to take away potential evidence, but it's just as likely to be trophy-hunting, whereby the killer keeps something from each victim. In ripper killers, the mutilation of the victim's body suggests that trophy-hunting is far more compelling.

So what really makes a ripper killer? Experts, including Dr Joel Norris, who has written a number of books on serial killers including *Serial Killers* and *Jeffrey Dahmer*, believe that there are seven steps for the perpetrators of serial and ripper killings. The first involves the "aura phase", where the perpetrator's senses are increasingly heightened, and antisocial tendencies take over. This is when the killer will need to identify his next victim. The hatred and anger felt by the killer at this time are unparalleled. Often seen in those who stalk people over the internet, the trolling phase comes next, where the victim is sought, with the killer focusing on venues that will provide them with their next kill. Trolling is not random or accidental – ripper killers know exactly where to find their victims. Phase three involves "wooing" the victim into trusting the perpetrator, so that they can be lured to a suitable spot. The next phase is the capture phase, where the trap is sprung. This may be in the form of stunning the victim. Next the actual murder itself takes place, and provides the emotional "high" for the killer. The "trophy" phase is when the murderer will take something that belongs to the victim, so that the crime can be relived over and over again. Body parts of victims are often taken by ripper killers in the same way that a game hunter might take the head of an animal, but jewellery belonging to the murdered woman, underwear or other items, also constitute trophies. Along with the "high", comes the "low", and ripper killers are often quite depressed following a murder. The final phase brings the killer to an all-time low, and this is what triggers the perpetrator to "hunt" again. Ripper killers are quite often fixated on the domination, cruelty and mutilation of their victims, and there can be a reluctance to form social and emotional bonds with others, especially women. As a result, these perpetrators turn to fantasy as a means of escaping their lives, in which they may be dominated by an emotionally stronger female, or may have been dominated by a woman in the past, while many also have poor self-esteem. Ripper killers tend to be paranoid and feel justified in their killings. Profilers of Jack the Ripper believe that he justified his killings as ridding society of worthless, heavy-drinking "unfortunates" who had little to offer the world. This book takes a look at some of the most notorious ripper killers from the past 100 years, and delves deep into their sinister lives and the deadly crimes they committed.

Jack the Ripper

1888

It's not true that Jack the Ripper was the first serial killer, or even the first ripper killer in history. A number of other dubious characters were known and written about hundreds of years before "Jack", as he was dubbed, brought panic and mayhem to the streets of London. However, he was the first ripper killer to be widely feared on the "hunting grounds" of Whitechapel in London's East End. While five victims are known to have died at the hands of Jack the Ripper in the Victorian era of the 19th century, it has always been suspected that there were more.

On 1st April 1888, *The People* published an article about "a desperate attempt" to murder a young dressmaker at Bow, in the East End. The small thoroughfare of Burdett Road, lying midway between the East India Dock Road and Bow Road, was pierced by the screams coming from nearby Maidman Street. Two policemen were called to the scene by two women who claimed a young woman was being murdered. Ada Wilson was found lying in the passageway close to her lodgings. She was bleeding profusely from a wound to her throat. A local doctor, named Wheeler, bound the woman's throat before she was sent to hospital in a critical condition. Ada Wilson recovered enough to give a description of her attacker. She had answered the door to a stranger, who first demanded money from her, and told her she would die if she did not hand over her cash. Ada refused to give the man money, so he took out a clasp-knife and stabbed her twice in the throat. Aged around 30, around 5ft 6in and with a sunburnt face, the stranger was wearing a dark coat, light trousers and a wideawake hat. Exactly one week later, the attacker had struck again.

Described as an "unfortunate", Emma Eliza Smith, from George Street, Spitalfields, had left home one Monday evening, only to return home around 5.00 a.m. the next morning suffering from terrible injuries. She was attacked and robbed, before being stabbed in the face and abdomen. Part of her ear was badly cut. While it's known that Emma had been drinking that night, she was not drunk enough to have no idea what was happening to her, or what she was saying, according to witnesses. The doctor who tended to Emma when she died a day later confirmed to the coroner that she had been drinking but wasn't intoxicated. Emma Smith had suffered terrible internal injuries. She had been attacked with a blunt instrument so forcefully that her peritoneum and other internal organs had been perforated. Whether she was a "Ripper" victim will never be known, but the victim did indicate that she had been attacked by a group of men. The official verdict was "willful murder by person, or persons unknown". Meanwhile, the "outrages" continued unabated.

John Reeves, of George Yard Buildings, Whitechapel, found the body of a woman lying in a pool of blood on the first-floor landing of his digs in early August 1888. Reeves called Constable Barrett and Dr Keeling, who examined the body, pronounced the woman dead, and cited that she had been brutally murdered. There were knife wounds on the woman's breasts and abdomen, with many other wounds elsewhere on her body. The woman wasn't a tenant of the building, was unknown to all residents and no one had heard anything during the night. Inspector Elliston, of the Commercial Street police station, placed the case in the hands of Inspector Reid of the Criminal Investigation Department. The identity of the woman remained a mystery. One witness hadn't seen the woman lying on the landing at 2.00 a.m. that morning, but a cab driver, another resident, had seen the body, and had assumed it was someone drunk. The woman was found to have 39 puncture wounds, nine of which were to her throat, 17 to her breasts, and her left lung had been penetrated in five places, and the right lung in two places. The heart had also been stabbed, the liver had received five punctures, while the spleen had been penetrated twice. Dr Timothy Keeling deduced that the wounds were made by at least three weapons, which included, but were not limited to, a dagger or sword-bayonet, a long, strong instrument and a penknife.

George Yard was the scene of a further murder just one week later. A woman was found with a bayonet wound to her left breast, and other injuries that had been inflicted by a knife. Martha Turner worked as a hawker, and had been seen in the company of a soldier on the night she died. "Pearly Poll", the witness, also known as Mary Ann Connolly, identified one of the soldiers, said to have been with Martha on the night she died, in a line-up, but he was exonerated after records showed he was in barracks at the time in question. For Inspector Reid, the mystery continued. Contrary to earlier newspaper reports, John Reeves and his wife had heard cries for help the night Martha was killed, coming from the corner of Wentworth and George Street at about 11.00 p.m. At 12.30 p.m. they were disturbed again by "dreadful shrieks" and cries of murder, but quarrels and screaming were commonplace in the area, which was frequented by a number of undesirables, so having investigated and seen nothing but some people arguing, they had retired to bed. Worse was to come, with the brutal death of Mary Ann Nichols, who was found murdered on 31st August 1888. It was to mark the "official" beginning of the work of a terrifying serial killer.

On 2nd September 1888, the newspapers were full of Mary's (also known as Polly) death. *The People* reported: "A Woman Found Hacked to Death." The article continued: "Scarcely have the horror and sensation caused by the discovery of the murdered woman in Whitechapel some short time ago had time to abate, when another discovery is made, which, for the brutality exercised on the victim, is even more glaringly outrageous and horrible". The crime was shrouded in mystery, and the police had no evidence to trace the perpetrator. Constable John Neil was walking down Buck's Row in Whitechapel at about 3.45 a.m. on Friday 31st August, when he discovered a woman lying at the side of the street. The brutal murder was shocking. The woman's throat had been cut so severely that her head was almost severed. There was a massive gaping wound that extended behind both ears, the victim's clothes were cut and saturated in blood, and revealed further extensive injuries. Mary Ann Nichols, as she would later be identified, was taken to Whitechapel mortuary. She had suffered terrible mutilation. As her clothes were removed, her horrific injuries became evident. It appeared that the large knife used in the attack had been thrust into her neck behind the left ear, and then thrust in a similar position behind the right ear, before being wrenched round with such force that the victim was virtually decapitated. The lower body wounds proved equally shocking. The knife had been thrust as low into the body as possible before being deliberately ripped up through her body to the breast, causing almost complete disembowelment. The knife had then been stabbed into the body under each breast and drawn down to the thighs in a zig zag fashion. Nothing like it had ever been witnessed in the Whitechapel mortuary before. *The People* indicated that whether the wounds in the body had been caused before the woman's throat was cut was impossible to say, however, it was clear that any of the wounds could have proved fatal. Mary Ann Nichols was unknown to police and it took a time to formally identify her body. Her clothing indicated she was poor – and some of her undergarments bore the mark of a workhouse. The mark on the third finger of her left hand led police to the conclusion that she had been married and her wedding ring forcibly removed. Her eyes were blackened and swollen, and there were marks on her face as though she had had a desperate struggle with her attacker. Some of her teeth had also been knocked out in the brutal assault. There had been no screams for help in a densely populated area of the East End, indicating that the attack had been so swift that the victim had had no chance to cry for help. No one was allowed inside the mortuary to see the body except the police surgeon and the policemen tasked with removing the victim's clothes. These were later laid out on the ground and it took a number of policemen to keep local children away from the scene around the mortuary. Nichols had been wearing her best stuff dress, and a rough brown ulster with large buttons, but her other clothes were extremely old, including her boots, which were split in many places. The way in which the clothes had been torn and cut was evidence of the brutal ferocity with which the deadly attack had been made. Inspector Helson of the Criminal Investigation Department, and Sergeants Enright and Godley headed up the case.

The only possessions found on the murdered woman were a broken comb and a piece of mirror. She was considered an "unfortunate" by police, who suspected that she spent her nights in common lodging houses. Police first set about making inquiries of various gangs known to operate in the local area. It was thought that the gangs, who only made their appearance in the early hours of the morning, had been blackmailing the woman and then killed her in a horrific way when she was unable to pay. Although police had been watching a number of gangs which operated in the area for some time, they had nothing to go on with regard to the murder of Nichols. It was believed, according to the newspaper, that with the prospect of a reward, and a free pardon, some of them may be willing to turn Queen's evidence. Buck's Row, a narrow passage running out of Thomas Street, contained about a dozen houses. It was suspected that the murder had been committed inside one of these dwellings before the victim was removed to the spot where she was discovered. The reason given for this insight was that some of the wounds would have been extremely difficult to inflict while the victim was dressed. While Nichols' clothes remained in the police yard, various locals came forward to identify them. At three o'clock on the afternoon of 31st August, a middle-aged woman identified them as belonging to "Polly", a woman who had lived for six weeks at a lodging house in Charles Street, but kept herself to herself. The woman said that Polly was married, and her husband still alive, and that she had a son aged 18. The woman also confirmed that Polly was living apart from her husband and did not like to be questioned about her personal circumstances.

By this time, the police were confident that they were dealing with a lunatic. They had no other theory to account for the horrendous murder. Local residents obviously felt the same way. It caused mayhem in Whitechapel. People were afraid to go outside, especially at night-time. The actual spot where the woman was found was continuously crowded with onlookers and police struggled to keep order. The bloodstains remained in the street, showing that the victim had possibly been carried some distance before being dumped. What police became fairly confident of within hours, despite the fact that Inspector Helson was struggling to find any traces of the "madman" at large, was that the murder was unlikely to have been carried out by more than one man. It was believed in the early days of the case that the weapon used was a butcher's knife. It was the third murder of a woman in the Whitechapel area in 12 months, and on the day after the murder,

Scotland Yard confirmed that no arrests had been made.

On 9th September 1888, another murder of a woman was discovered. It came just one week after the death of Mary Ann Nichols. The body of the victim was found early in the morning in the back yard, at the foot of a passage leading to a lodging house in Old Brown's Lane, Spitalfields. Emilia Richardson, who owned the house, always left the door to the passage open for the convenience of her lodgers. The murdered woman was found by Mr Davis, a resident on the second floor, as he left for work in the early morning. She was lying on her back, close to the flight of steps leading into the yard. Her throat was cut so deeply that the murderer had tied a handkerchief round it so that the head would not become detached from the body. The woman's body had also been completely ripped open and her heart and other organs were placed on the pavement by her side. The murderer had tied entrails round the victim's neck, and thick clots of blood were found next to the body. It appeared that the woman had been murdered in the street and then placed in the passage, borne out by the trail of blood from the road to where she was found. There were no signs of a struggle. Mr Davis summoned police from Commercial Street station as soon as he made his grisly discovery, and despite the early hour, there was a great deal of panic in the local area. A crowd began to gather around Mrs Richardson's house, as well as outside the mortuary, to where the body had been removed. The woman appeared to be roughly the same age as Mary Ann Nichols – around 45 – and there were signs that a ring had been wrenched from the third finger of the victim's left hand. The 5ft woman was dressed in lace-up boots and striped stockings. She wore two cotton petticoats and was respectably dressed. Nothing was found in her pockets except a handkerchief and two small combs. Rumours were rife, including the fact that a leather apron and a long knife were found near the place where the body had been discovered, which it was cited belonged to a local man known as "Leather Apron", for whom police were already searching following the previous murder. By this time, the police were confident that they were dealing with the same perpetrator, and this murder gave them, according to newspaper reports, more evidence than they'd managed to gain in the previous five months of ongoing attacks. However, the crimes were still shrouded in mystery.

As the crowds began to dissipate in the late morning, a young man, about 25 years old, was seen running down Commercial Street followed by a considerable body of policemen with drawn batons, and a huge crowd of locals, before he was grabbed by a large man, who blocked his way as he scarpered down a side street. The pursuers were kept at bay by police as the man was apprehended and taken to Commercial Street police station. It then transpired that the discovery of a leather apron had been nothing but a rumour, however, there had been one hanging on a peg in the passageway, but which had no obvious connection to the murder.

With the advent of a serial killer on the loose, Frederick Abberline, Henry Moore and Walter Andrews were seconded from the Central Office at Scotland Yard. *The People* reported: "At the adjourned inquiry, at the Working Lads' Institute, Whitechapel, into the circumstances attending the death of Mary Ann Nichols, aged 42, whose body, terribly mutilated, was found in Buck's Row. Whitechapel Inspectors Helson and Abberline attended for the police, and Detective Sergeant Enright, of Scotland Yard, was also present – Inspector Spratling, of the J Division, deposed that at about four o'clock on Friday morning, the 31st August, while in Hackney Road, he received information as to the finding of the body of the deceased. Before he reached the spot the body had been removed to the mortuary. While he was taking a description there he discovered the injuries to the abdomen, and at once sent for Dr. Llewellyn. While describing the clothes which were on the body, the witness said the corsets had no cuts on them". While the corsets were fastened, there was no conclusive witness statement as to whether they were done up at the back or the front when found on the victim. The doctor was also unable to state to the coroner whether there were any cuts in the woman's clothing that correlated to her injuries because he had not examined her garments. H. Tomkins, from Coventry Street, Bethnal Green, said he was at work at the slaughterhouse in Winthorpe Street and left work about 4.00 a.m. on the Friday morning. He was approaching Buck's Row when a constable told him of the murder. None of the men working that night at the slaughterhouse had left the building between 1.00 a.m. and 4.00 a.m. and none had heard anything unusual. Inspector Helson was called next to give evidence and said: "At 6.45 on the morning of the 31st, at my house, I received information of the affair. I first went to Bethnal Green police station and made myself acquainted with the facts, after which I went to the mortuary. The body was fully dressed, except the bonnet. The bodice of the dress was open for about four buttons from the top. They might have been undone by the doctor. The stays were shorter than usual, and did not reach the hip. There were no blood marks on either of the petticoats. The back of the dress just about the shoulders was soaked in blood, which had flowed from the wound in the neck. The ulster was also saturated, and between that and the dress the blood was clotted. The other parts of the body were clean, but did not give one the impression that the body had been recently washed. The face was bruised, as if by a blow on the cheek, and the right jaw appeared to have been struck. There were no marks of any ring being torn off her finger, and there was no evidence of any struggle having taken place. All the injuries could have been inflicted while the woman was wearing her clothes. I have examined the spot where the body was found in Buck's Row. There were no signs of blood on the large gates where the body was laid, and as the paint was fresh, they would, had they been there, have been easily visible. I should say that the outrage was committed on the spot." Other witnesses were called before the coroner adjourned the inquest to allow the police more time to carry out their inquiries and the jury was disbanded. As the days passed, police were clear that both Mary Ann Nichols and the later victim had been killed brutally by the same man. The murder of a woman in Rainham in 1887 was also cited as possibly being linked. The victim had been dismembered, and different parts of her body thrown into the River Thames. The injuries to her abdominal walls were similar to the two cases now linked by police. All three crimes, and those committed earlier than the murder of Nichols, appeared to have been carried out by someone who had a familiarity with anatomy and skill in using a knife. One witness who came forward at the time of Nichols' death was Harriet Lilley, who lived two doors away from where the victim was found in Buck's Row, and who had been unable to sleep on the night of the murder. She had heard a painful moan, followed by two or three gasps, before the noise had stopped. At around this time, Mrs Lilley had heard a goods train on the East London Railway at about half past three, out from New Cross, which was the time that the victim was either killed, or placed in Buck's Row. In early September, police were still hunting for Leather Apron, who was known to have threatened and abused a number of women in the local area. However, whether he was actually involved in the murders had yet to be ascertained. He was described by the newspaper as: "Aged 30 years, height, 5ft. 3in, complexion, dark, sallow, hair and moustache, black, thick set, dressed in old and dirty clothing, and is of Jewish appearance". Nichols, it was stated, had been seen in the company of this man just hours before her death, and if nothing else, he might be a vital witness. Mary Ann Nichols was buried on 6th September 1888 in a simple service. Thousands turned out to see the woman take her final journey. The two-horse hearse was eventually spotted being driven down Hanbury Street. Mourners were prevented from getting too close by police from H Division, much to their frustration. The hearse made its way towards Ilford accompanied by the victim's father, two of her children and her nephew, who received much sympathy from onlookers.

On 16th September 1888, it was reported that a further arrest had been made and the prisoner detained in custody. The man had been reported as acting suspiciously in the neighbourhood of Flower and Dean Street. He was eventually sent to the workhouse infirmary as being: "an individual of unsound mind". He was known to have carried several large butchers' knives and even his friends were indifferent towards him. It was established that his movements over the previous two months would have to be investigated, as he'd been missing from his home during that time and no one knew of his whereabouts or activities. At the same time, it appeared that vital evidence was being withheld from police by women associates of the previous two victims, mainly because they were completely convinced that should they help with inquiries they would suffer the same fate and several women had left the Whitechapel area altogether. Pensioner Edward Stanley, known to frequent the company of Annie Chapman, the second victim, was the next witness to attend Commercial Street police station, where he made a statement to Inspector Helson. He was proved not to be connected to the murders in any way, having given a satisfactory explanation for his whereabouts. He had known the victim for about two years and stated to police that she had no "quarrelsome" relationships with men as far as he was aware.

During mid-September, there was some surprise that the witness statement of Mr Cadoche, who lived next door to 29 Hanbury Street where Annie's body was found in the yard, had not been included at the inquest. Cadoche had passed the wooden partition between his own lodgings and number 29, on his way to and from using the outside lavatory. He heard a woman say: "No, no," as he made his way past the fence, and on his way back heard a scuffle before someone fell against the partition. There was no cry for help and the witness quietly made his way inside. Further inquiries revealed that the four murdered women were known to one another, but other women still failed to feel safe in coming forward with evidence. However, several women reported seeing a man with a knife in the local area, which further fuelled the panic in Whitechapel. The man these women described was short in stature, with a sandy beard and wore a cloth cap. On one occasion he was pursued by a number of men who were alerted by a witness, but he disappeared up a side street. The description of the man also coincided with witness statements from Flower and Dean Street by another woman, who saw him carrying a large knife. He had behaved extremely strangely. As a result, Edward McKenna was apprehended by police. He was found with a small table knife in a drunken state, but he protested his innocence and said the knife was for cutting his food. Although the police did not attach great importance to the arrest, they detained him while they pursued their inquiries. Leather Apron, named as John Piser, a shoemaker, was also questioned in connection with the murders, but released without charge. Dr George Bagster Phillips, who carried out the post-mortem on Annie Chapman, stated at the inquest that her tongue was swollen, and although he had seen the victim with her intestines lying on the ground and around her shoulder, he noticed under further examination that she had had her breathing compromised before death. In other words, she had been strangled. It was also clear that the murderer had attempted to separate the vertebral bone from the neck. There were other mutilations, which the doctor stated he felt were subsequent to the death of the victim. He ascertained that death was caused by syncope, or from heart failure due to loss of blood, caused by the severance of the throat. It was inflicted by a very sharp knife, with probably a thin, narrow blade, about six to eight inches long. Owing to the way in which the body was cut, there was evidence of anatomical knowledge by the murderer. Annie had a number of bruises on her body, which the doctor was confident were caused a few days prior to death. She had eaten a meal on the day she died, but showed no signs of heavy drinking, for which she was allegedly renowned.

That same week, a little girl was passing by the back yard of number 25 Hanbury Street, and found peculiar marks on the wall and the garden fence. Detective Inspector Chandler, who was at the house making a plan of the back gardens on the street, carefully examined the child's find and discovered that the bloody trail ran five to six feet in the direction of the back door of number 25. There was no doubt that the trail was that of the murderer, who, it was evident, had passed through or over the fence between numbers 29 and 27 before entering the garden of number 25. On the wall of the last house there was a curious mark, between a smear and a sprinkle, which was probably made by the murderer as he banged his blood-soaked coat against the wall. The yard backed onto the works of a packing-case maker called Bailey, and in the yard, in a corner, the police found some crumpled paper saturated with blood. It was obvious to the authorities that the murderer had wiped his hands on the paper before throwing it over the wall into the works' yard. The doors to number 25, and the passageway to the back yard were always left open for the benefit of the tenants and police suspected that the murderer had planned his getaway through the building and onto the street.

The funeral of Annie Chapman took place early on Friday 14th September 1888. *The People* stated: "The utmost secrecy was observed in the arrangements, and none but the undertaker, the police, and the relatives of the deceased knew anything about it. Shortly after seven o'clock a hearse drew up outside the mortuary in Montagu-street, and the body was quickly removed. At nine o'clock a start was made for Manor Park Cemetery, the place selected by the friends of the deceased for the interment, but no coaches followed, as it was desired that public attention should not be attracted. Mr Smith and other relatives met the body at the cemetery, and the service was duly performed in the ordinary manner. The remains of the deceased were enclosed in a black covered elm coffin, which bore the words, 'Annie Chapman, died September the 8th, 1888, aged 48 years.'"

Within a few short weeks, four murders had been committed within the Whitechapel district of East London. The first victim had had an iron stake driven through her body, the second was stabbed more than 30 times, but Nichols and Chapman were the victims who were most horrifically murdered and mutilated in a terrible rage by the unknown assailant dubbed Jack the Ripper. Chapman's injuries were even more shocking than Nichols' and yet the mystery continued with police no nearer to apprehending the unknown ripper killer. Newspapers at the time were convinced that the murders were the work of one "madman". Each murder had taken place within a short distance from the others, and all the victims had been killed in the early hours of the morning, when the streets were deserted. All the victims were described as "unfortunate", and no plausible motive had yet been established. It was also cited that if a gang were involved then more evidence would have surely come to light by this time because at least one member of a blood-letting group would have come forward. *The People* said: "But one man, bent upon keeping his own counsel with all the cunning of a homicidal maniac, will certainly never betray his fatal secret by any voluntary action." Apart from 1812 and the famous East End murders, Whitechapel had never seen a frenzy like it. The idea that the mysterious murderer was walking in their midst had local residents in total panic, which, combined with the fact that the police appeared powerless to do anything to stop the maniac, really frightened everyone in the vicinity. Many men were arrested on suspicion of the murders, but all were released. The man they were ultimately searching for would have had to walk down Hanbury Street, covered in blood, while workmen walked their weary way to jobs across the district. Police suspected that the murderer had to be living close by, or he would never have been able to escape undetected. "The East End, and London in general, will not rest easy until the shadow of this great terror is removed from our streets," said the paper. The police were praised for their efforts, but there was genuine frustration at the lack of progress that was fuelling the fear in Whitechapel. The reporter on *The People* said: "The fact is, that there are not enough policemen, or anything like enough, to do the duty that has to be done in London. Five million human beings, including the most desperate criminal class in the world, need more than twelve thousand policemen, all told, to maintain public order and to prevent such tragedies as those in Whitechapel. How many people, we should be curious to know, who sneer at the police and complain of inefficient police protection, are aware of the actual proportion of the numbers of the metropolitan police to the numbers of the metropolitan public? But, if the police have been unable to prevent the murderer from accomplishing his sanguinary work, it is all the more absolutely imperative that they should succeed in bringing him to justice and to the gallows, which is too good for him."

Less than two weeks after Annie's funeral another woman died in brutal circumstances. By this time (the end of September 1888), the crimes were being dubbed "The Whitechapel Murders", while it became clear that there was also a market for human organs. An American man had made a request to the authorities of more than one of the London hospitals for a number of specimens, including the organs which had been found to be missing from Chapman's body. The man had offered up to £20 per organ. It led, at least for a time, to the belief that the murderer was "hunting" to order. The murderer had compressed the throat of each victim so they were unable to cry out, but had been unable to collect the desired body parts from Mary Ann Nichols, probably because he was interrupted in the act. The victims' tongues were swollen, perhaps as a sign of suffocation. As a result, and the fact that earlier murder victims had been hacked and mutilated in blind and savage fury, it was deemed that Nichols was the first "true" victim of Jack the Ripper, the madman terrorizing London's East End. The way in which Annie Chapman's body was harvested led police and the authorities to believe that she was killed by someone familiar with the post-mortem room, perhaps a doctor. The skill shown when removing the woman's uterus, upper section of the vagina and posterior two-thirds of the bladder was a clear indication that the murderer knew exactly what he was doing. John Fitzgerald, who gave himself up at Wandsworth police station for the murder of Annie Chapman, had his story discredited in late September 1888.

By 7th October 1888, the news was full of murder again. This time, two women had been brutally killed. On Sunday 30th September, Elizabeth Stride was found murdered around 1.00 a.m. When the usual edition of *The People* went to press that morning, little did the newspaper know that within a few hours they would be called to chronicle two more atrocities. The news at that time had failed to reach the Strand, but by late morning and that afternoon, journalists were clamouring to get the latest on the Whitechapel murders.

In Berner Street, a narrow, badly-lit, but respectable thoroughfare, turning out of Commercial Road, a short distance down on the right-hand side away from Whitechapel, the London School Board sat opposite what was known as an "International and Educational Club", held in a private house. This stood at the corner of a gateway leading into a yard in which were small manufacturing premises and four small houses. The yard gates were usually closed at night, with a wicket giving admission to the lodgers and others residing in the houses. The club had held an evening lecture on Judaism and Socialism, which was followed by a discussion. A sing-song ended the evening around 12.30 a.m., and no cries for help outside were heard by those attending the event. The steward of the club had returned to his house in the yard with his cart, before discovering an object lying in his way as he turned into the gateway. He lit a match to get a better view of the bundle lying under the wall and discovered it to be a woman. He thought at first she was drunk and called out to other members of the club who found her head almost severed from her body when they lit more lights to enable them to see more clearly. Blood was streaming into the gutter. When the body was removed, it was found that only the throat had been cut and there was no mutilation to the abdomen as there had been with the first two ripper victims. However, police suspected that the killer had been interrupted. The steward's cart, pulled by a donkey, had not long drawn into the street, and it was deemed that this had put a halt to any dismemberment or mutilation of the victim's body. Police believed that the murderer had thrown his victim to the ground before cutting her throat from ear to ear. Just 45 minutes later, another victim faced a terrible death at the hands of the ripper killer.

The first victim that night was also known as "Long Liz". Born in Sweden 44 years earlier, the woman had lived with Thomas Bates and his wife in lodgings for five or six years. She lied to the couple and said that her husband and children had all been drowned on a sinking ship some years before, but in fact, she had separated from her husband and had no children who were drowned. Stride was hard-working, and generally kept herself to herself. She mainly worked as a cleaning lady, or charwoman, but did work the streets when absolutely necessary. She was a popular woman, who had been absent for quite some time before returning to London just prior to her death. Stride was known to go away for extended periods, but those in the same lodgings were always glad to welcome her back. On the evening of her murder she had left home at around 7.00 p.m. The second victim that night was found just after 2.00 a.m. in Mitre Square, Aldgate, within the City boundaries but on the outskirts of Whitechapel. She was found by Constable Watkins of the City Police as he made his rounds, apparently lifeless, in a pool of blood. He immediately blew his whistle. Inspector Collard quickly arrived, followed by surgeon, Mr G W Sequeira and Dr Gordon Brown, the divisional police doctor from Finsbury Circus. The woman was dead, lying on her back, with her head inclined to the left. Her left leg was extended, her right leg was bent, and both her arms were extended. Her throat was severed and there was a large gash across her face from the nose to the right angle of the cheek, and part of the right ear had been cut off. There were further mutilations to the lower part of the victim's body, which appeared to have been carried out more rapidly and roughly than in the cases of Nichols and Chapman. The victim was removed to the mortuary in Golden Lane. Both her eyes had been damaged, particularly the right one, which appeared to have been "smashed in". The 5ft victim, with auburn hair, wore a black cloth jacket, a dark green print dress, a thin white vest, an old green alpaca petticoat, white chemise, a drab linsey skirt, brown ribbed stockings mended at the feet with white material and a black bonnet of straw. She also carried a white bone-handled table knife, two short clay pipes, a red cigarette case, a piece of string, a white handkerchief and a matchbox with cotton in it. The constable was adamant that the body had not been where he found it for more than 15 minutes. It was strongly believed that the victim and "Jack" had watched the policeman round the corner of the square before entering. As the mutilation was particularly rough, doctors cited that it could have been done in five minutes, allowing the killer to make his escape before the policeman returned while still on his beat. Mitre Square was surrounded by narrow streets leading from it and police suspected that the woman was killed on the ground, so the killer was able to leave quickly undetected without having been too blood-stained. There would have been a market in Middlesex Street (formerly Petticoat Lane) that Sunday morning, and a watchman was working directly opposite the murder scene, while a policeman was sleeping in another part of the square. The murderer must have quickly overcome his victim before carrying out a horrific crime of "extraordinary daring and brutality". A witness spotted a man of fair complexion, aged 35 to 40, throwing a woman to the ground, but deciding it was a husband and wife having a quarrel, had thought no more of it. A man matching the same description had been into a pub in Batty Street at 10.30 p.m. and heard regulars talking about the Whitechapel murderer. The man had joined in the conversation saying that he personally knew the murderer and that the drinkers would hear about Jack the Ripper the following day, which of course, they did. One of the most important witness statements came from someone claiming that an American man was reported to have been seen in Bow Road loitering about in a suspicious manner, but left the area once he discovered he was being watched.

A postcard, bearing the stamp: "London, E., October 1st," was received on Monday morning addressed to the Central News Office. Written in red and undoubtedly having come from the same person from whom a sensational letter had been received the previous week, the postcard made reference to the murders and provided a sequel to the first letter. It said: "I was not codding, dear old Boss, when I gave you the tip. You'll hear about Saucy Jacky's work to-morrow. Double event this time. Number one squealed a bit; couldn't finish straight off. Had not time to get ears for police. Thanks for keeping last letter back till I got to work again. Jack The Ripper."

The postcard was smeared both sides with blood, which had been added by the thumb or finger of the writer. Some words were almost obliterated by a bloody smear. The *Central News* added in its article of 7th October that the communication was being taken as a hoax. However, at the same time, the news office was inclined to think, given the contents of the first letter, that the murderer was playing a practical joke on them. It read: "September 25th, 1888 – Dear Boss, I keep on hearing the police have caught me, but they won't fix me just yet. I have laughed when they look so clever, and talk about being on the right track. Great joke about Leather Apron. Gave me real fits. I am down on – and I shan't quit ripping them till I do get buckled. Grand work the last job. I gave the lady no time to squeal. How can they catch me now? I love my work and want to start again. You will soon hear of me with my funny little games. I saved some of the proper red stuff in a singer-beer bottle over the last job to write with, but it went thick, like glue, and I can't use it. Red ink is fit enough, I hope. Ha, ha! The next job I do I shall clip the lady's ears off and send to the police officers, just for jolly – wouldn't you? Keep this letter back till I do a bit more work, then give it out straight. My knife's so nice and sharp. I want to get to work right away if I get a chance. Good luck. Yours truly, JACK THE RIPPER. Don't mind giving me the trade name. Wasn't good enough to post this before I got all the red ink off my hands; curse it. No luck yet. They say I'm a doctor now. Ha, ha!"

By the Tuesday following the murders on Sunday 30th September, numerous callers had stopped at the mortuary on Golden Lane to see the unidentified woman. The police were by now convinced that the murderer had had a very narrow escape from being caught in the act of killing Elizabeth Stride in Berner Street. The fact that the donkey and cart had pulled into the street and then the yard suggests that their arrival coincided with the murder taking place and that the killer mingled with members of the club as they rushed out to see the body of the victim before he made his escape. The press agreed with the police that the theory was at least plausible.

Whitechapel became panic-stricken following the two further murders. While crowds of people still thronged the main streets until the public houses shut, once the small hours arrived, the thoroughfares of London's East End were deserted. Unfortunate women, who would normally walk the streets at this time, were noticeably absent according to newspaper reports. Coffee stall keepers had little option but to sit and wait while their all-night customers remained elusive. All knew they had lost their business to "the murders". The only people pounding the streets in the days following the late September killings were reporters looking for a story and lonely policemen on the beat.

Meanwhile, Professor J Wortley Axe, principal of the Royal Veterinary College in London, told reporters that he favoured the use of bloodhounds in trying to flush out the murderer. All dogs have a natural instinct for blood odours, but training would be required if dogs were to prove useful to the case. However, Professor Axe was mindful that in a large city with many inhabitants, the job would prove much harder than in the countryside where ground lay undisturbed for longer periods of time.

Two weeks after the third and fourth ripper murders, police were despondent. They had made an increasing number of arrests, and interviewed many more suspects, but none of these men were the perpetrator. By now, police knew the fourth victim as Catherine Eddowes, an unfortunate woman, originally from Wolverhampton, who had moved to London with her family as a child. Both Stride and Eddowes had been in police custody the night they died. Both had been held in a cell while they sobered up from drinking. However, the police turned the two half-drunk women out into the night, to face a terrifying death. Stride was released around midnight, while Eddowes left another station at about 1.00 a.m., just under an hour before she was killed. She was last seen alive by traveller Joseph Lewende at around 1.30 a.m. as he left the Imperial Club in Duke Street with some friends. His statement was corroborated by his friend, another witness, Joseph Levy, a butcher from Aldgate. Written on a wall, near the victim, were the words: "The Jews are the men that will not be blamed for nothing". This writing was quickly removed, rather than being protected by police until it could be examined further. The coroner mentioned that it should have been preserved as part of the evidence, just in case it was connected to the murder, at the inquest in October 1888. The inquest concluded, following witness statements from medical professionals, that Eddowes had not been mutilated by a murderer with much anatomical knowledge and that no organs had been removed from the body. Annie Phillips, daughter of Catherine Eddowes, was also called as a witness. She told the jury that she was on good terms with her mother, but usually only saw her when the older woman needed money. She had not seen her mother for around 18 months prior to the murder. Catherine Eddowes was buried in Ilford cemetery.

On 16th October 1888, George Akin Lusk, a builder and prominent member of the Whitechapel Vigilance Committee, received a parcel, which contained a portion of a kidney. The box and its contents were taken to Leman Street, to the City Police Office in Old Jewry, where it was examined by Dr Gordon Brown, the police surgeon. One curator of the Pathological Museum at the London Hospital believed that the partial human organ had been preserved in spirits for up to 10 days. Meanwhile, police denied that they had arrested an American in Bermondsey, and a strange man was observed writing "I am Jack the Ripper", on a wall in Islington. He was pursued, but managed to evade those chasing him. Catherine Eddowes had been found to be missing her left kidney during a post-mortem. The partial kidney sent to Mr Lusk was believed to be that of the ripper's fourth victim. The letter sent inside the box with the kidney showed the same handwriting as another postcard sent to the Central News Office, just a few days before. It read: "Say Boss, – You seem rare frightened, guess I'd like to give you fits, but can't stop time enough to let you box of toys play copper games with me, but hope to see you when I don't hurry to much. Bye-bye, Boss." Meanwhile, the letter to Lusk read: "From Hell. Mr Lusk, Sir, I send you half the kidney I took from one woman preserved it for you together [with a] piece I fried and ate it was very nice I may send you the bloody knife that took it out if you only wate [sic] while longer. Signed Catch me when you can Mishter Lusk." The letter was not signed Jack the Ripper.

The arrests of suspects continued in Whitechapel, and in the third week in October it transpired that from the morning of the murders in Berner Street and Mitre Square, the police had been in possession of a man's shirt, saturated with blood. It was left at number 22 Batty Street, where the man in question had asked his landlady to wash it while he was away. The shirt, and the man were apprehended, and the landlady prevented from making any statement to the press. However, a reporter did manage to interview the woman, who confirmed that her lodger was a ladies' tailor, working for a West End house. Meanwhile, a man named Benjamin Graham was charged following his confession at the Guildhall Police Court with having committed the Whitechapel murders. He was charged on remand, but found to be intoxicated, and not insane. He was later discharged, without any means of punishment, although the authorities regretted that they could not charge him for wasting their time.

Things were quiet in Whitechapel for a time, but in early November, it was all over the newspapers that the "assassin" had reappeared. Matthew Packer, a fruit shop owner on Berner Street, had reported the man he had seen buying grapes for Elizabeth Stride the night she died. He had seen the man before, and the deceased, but hadn't seen the man in a while until early November. Packer was so spooked by the man who watched him menacingly that he feared for his life. He strongly believed that the man would stab him so that he could not identify him to the police. As Packer called for help from the nearby shoeblack, the man ran from the vicinity as fast as he could and managed to catch a passing tram. Dr Forbes Winslow, a leading authority in psychiatry in London, was still convinced that Jack the Ripper was a homicidal lunatic who had probably been through a "lucid" period, hence his disappearance for a few weeks.

While many of the hundreds of letters sent to police were considered to be hoaxes, there were others that were considered genuine at the time, including the ones to "Boss". The Poplar police station received the following in early November: "October 30th, 1888, Dear Boss, I am going to commit three more murders, two women and a child, and I shall take their hearts this time. – Yours truly (signed) JACK THE RIPPER." In the meantime, two knives were discovered in Kensington, and one bore signs of blood. They were found in the garden of a house in Harrington Gardens. Police had had the knives for a while, but decided to make the news public in November. They were found to be Gurkha knives, known as kukri, while the bloodstains were ascertained to be at least a month old, but not more than six to eight weeks old. The fact that the murderer may be hiding out in Kensington caused panic in the local vicinity.

On 11th November 1888, the newspaper headlines ran: "ANOTHER FIENDISH MURDER IN WHITECHAPEL. A Woman Cut to Pieces. Sickening Mutilation. Organs of the Body Missing. Panic in the District". It was the seventh murder within a matter of months, and the fifth murder that would be officially attributed to Jack the Ripper. The woman was described as another "unfortunate", who "occupied a miserably-furnished room in a court off Dorset Street, a narrow thoroughfare running out of Commercial Street, not far removed from the police station." The woman wasn't widely known locally, and those who were acquainted said her name was Mary Jane Kelly, or Mary Jane Fisher. Married with a little boy, Kelly was living apart from her husband. She had been seen regularly walking in the company of men, and it was supposed that she met her attacker late at night and felt comfortable enough to invite him home, or to allow him home with her. On the morning of her death, Mary Jane had been seen walking along Dorset Street at around 8.00 a.m., perhaps to buy food for breakfast. Three hours later, she was found lying in her bedroom in a pool of blood, having been badly mutilated. The discovery of her body was far more shocking than any of the previous murders, and was undoubtedly the work of Jack the Ripper. The killer had had the time to carry out his dubious "work" without fear of interruption. He was indoors, and no passers-by could surprise him, or stop him in his tracks. Mary Jane was found naked on the bed, with her head virtually severed from her body. It was attached by a thin piece of skin. Her abdomen was ripped open, both breasts had been slashed off, and the nose and ears were both missing. The flesh on the legs had been cut off in strips, leaving the bones of the thighs exposed. The face of the victim had also been "hacked", and pieces of flesh lay scattered around the room. On the table lay strips of flesh, the two breasts, and other portions of the deceased's body. The uterus and other organs, as in previous murders, had been removed. A portion of the entrails had been deliberately placed between the victim's legs, and one of her hands had been thrust into the gaping wound in the abdomen. Police were shocked at the discovery.

Dorset Street ran between Whitechapel and Shoreditch. It was half composed of warehouses, while the other half provided lodging houses. Kelly had owed her landlord and landlady several weeks' rent. At 11.00 a.m. on 9th November, she was found by John McCarthy's "man", who had been sent to collect the unpaid rent. He knocked on the door, but when he received no answer, he looked through the window from outside. The window was broken and using his hand, he was able to draw back the curtain and make the grisly discovery. He immediately called Mr McCarthy, who sent him to the police station. He returned with Inspector Back, who sent a telegram to Superintendent Arnold, but Inspector Abberline arrived on the scene first. John McCarthy said: "The poor woman's body was lying on the bed, undressed. She had been completely disembowelled, and her entrails had been taken out and placed on the table ... The woman's nose had been cut off, and her face gashed and mutilated, so that she was quite beyond recognition. Both her breasts, too, had been clean cut away and placed by the side of her liver and other entrails on the table. I had heard a great deal about the Whitechapel murders, but ... I had never expected to see such a sight as this."

Even doctors called to the scene were appalled at what they witnessed that day. The crime was extremely barbaric according to reports, but medical doctors were of the same opinion, "that the murderer possessed some anatomical knowledge". It then transpired that Annie Chapman and Mary Jane Kelly had been friends.

A young woman who sold roasted chestnuts on the corner of Widegate Street, just two minutes' walk from the murder scene, came forward to tell police how she saw a man at around midday dressed like a gentleman, who approached her and said: "I suppose you have heard about the murder in Dorset Street?" She replied that she had and he then smiled at her and said: "I know more about it than you." He then stared into her face before walking away, but he looked back to check if she was watching him. She gave a different description of this man than that of the short man with the fair moustache that most other witnesses had given in previous murders. The man, she recounted, had a black moustache, was about 5ft 6in tall, and wore a black silk hat, a black coat, and speckled trousers. He carried a black shiny bag, about a foot in depth, and a foot and a half in length. The woman had seen the man the night before the murder when he was accosted by three "unfortunate" girls, who asked him what he carried in the bag. The woman said in her statement that he had replied: "Something that the ladies don't like." There was nothing at all to suspect that the young woman on the chestnut stall was anything but genuine.

The daring of the murderer was unprecedented, and another letter reached the police. It read: "Dear Boss, I shall be busy to-morrow night in Marylebone-road. I have booked two for blood. Yours, JACK THE RIPPER. Look out about two o'clock in Marylebone-road." More and more arrests followed, including that of Joe Barnett, with whom Kelly had lived, but none, it seemed, were the ripper killer terrorizing London. Meanwhile, 27-year-old Thomas Bowyer told the inquest how he had found Mary Jane Kelly's body after John McCarthy had asked him to collect the unfortunate woman's rent. He described in great detail the horror he had witnessed when peering through the window at the woman lying dead on the bed. Following all witness statements, the inquest returned a verdict that Mary Jane Kelly had been willfully murdered by "some person, or persons unknown".

The final ripper victim was buried on Monday 19th November in the Roman Catholic Cemetery at Leytonstone. On the coffin were two crowns of artificial flowers, and a cross made of heartsease. An enormous crowd completely blocked the street, but police kept order as the coffin was carried by four men to an open car. *The People* wrote: "The crowd was greatly moved ... Women with faces streaming with tears cried out: 'God forgive her!' and every man's head was bared. The sight was remarkable, and the emotion natural and unconstrained. Two mourning coaches followed, one containing three, and the other five persons. Joe Barnett was amongst them, with some one from McCarthy's, the landlord; and the others were women who had given evidence at the inquest ... The Rev Father Columban, with two acolytes and a cross bearer, met the body at the door of the little chapel of St Patrick, and the coffin was carried at once to a grave in the north-eastern corner."

The furore over Jack the Ripper continued unabated for a number of years after the death of Mary Jane Kelly. There were no similar murders for at least six months after the funeral of the 25-year-old, and many believed that the ripper killer had stopped either because he had died, was incarcerated, emigrated or was institutionalized. The last reports from *The People* about the Whitechapel murders came in March 1891, but there have been thousands of words written about Jack the Ripper ever since the first reported murders in 1888. It was suggested in the 1960s, "tongue in cheek" that he suffered from "moon madness", and his letters, postcards and sketches were published in April 1966, nearly 80 years after the murders. A civil servant, Brian Reilly, believed he had uncovered the identity of the ripper in 1972, and gave a dossier in which he claimed that the notorious murderer was a London doctor serving the City of London police. He named his suspect as Dr Merchant, having read a book written by Police Constable Robert Spicer, who claimed he had arrested the ripper. Dr Merchant was found to have been practicing at the time in Brixton, but police let him go without checking in his black bag. He died in 1890, not long after the final murder, and was cited as dying from a tubercular ulcer, which doctors at the time believed was a condition that the ripper killer suffered from. At the time of the murders, says the *Mirror* in 1988: "A million outcast people packed the disease ridden slums of Whitechapel. There were 1,200 prostitutes of the lowest kind willing to stand against a wall of a reeking back yard for the price of a doss or a quart of rot-gut gin. These were the Ripper's victims." The article by Murray Davies continues: "At the peak of the terror, police were receiving 100 letters a week ... Interestingly, the only letter believed genuine – the one enclosing the kidney – was not signed Jack the Ripper." Murray claims that "Jack" refused to accept his public name. He also names another man as the possible ripper, Montague John Druitt, a failed barrister from a medical family who believed he was going insane. He drowned himself in the Thames in December 1888. Sir Melville Macnaghten – who joined Scotland Yard in 1889 – made him the number one suspect and wrote in private papers: "He was sexually insane and from private information I have little doubt but that his own family believed him to have been the murderer." However, he also suspected Russian doctor Michael Ostrog, who was later held in a lunatic asylum as a homicidal maniac and a man named Kosminski, from Poland, who lived in Whitechapel and who also went insane, "owing to many years' indulgence in solitary vice". The Duke of Clarence, the eldest son of King Edward VII was even suspected at some point of being "Jack", but his misogynist tutor, James Stephen, as well as royal doctor, Sir William Gull, were all thought to have been possible suspects too. George Chapman (real name, Severin Klosowski), a medical student and barber who worked in Whitechapel, was one of the prime suspects. He was hanged in 1903 for having poisoned three wives. But author Donald Rumblelow said: "I have always had the feeling that on the Day of Judgement, when the real Jack the Ripper steps forward and calls out his true name, we experts will look blankly at each other and say, 'Who?'" He could well be right. In Australia, Professor Ian Findlay used powerful DNA-profiling techniques to examine the 118-year-old letters in 2006, which revealed that the ripper could have, in fact, been a woman. He said: "This is the most sophisticated DNA-fingerprinting technique in the world, but the sample doesn't give us enough evidence to pinpoint the killer. However, there is an interesting twist because we do know this sample is likely to be a female sample." Interestingly, Frederick Abberline was the one man who thought the ripper could be a woman. His boss doubted that a woman could be capable of such atrocious crimes, but Abberline remained unconvinced. The chief female suspect was Mary Pearcey. Born in 1866, she was executed at the scaffold in 1890 after being convicted of murdering her lover's wife and baby daughter. These murders bore striking similarities to the ripper killings. She was extremely strong with nerves of "iron cast", according to Macnaghten. Or, as others claim, was the ripper Whitechapel hospital doctor, Stephen Herbert Appleford? No one can be certain of anything without hard evidence, but one thing is for sure, the case of Jack the Ripper remains one of the greatest murder mysteries of all time.

The Berlin River Murders

1904

In June 1904, following a number of murders, a workman named Berger was arrested and accused of murdering a little girl called Lucie Berlin. There had been a series of crimes that bore similarities to Jack the Ripper's killings in Victorian Whitechapel in the 1880s, and Lucie's mutilated body was found in the River Spree. Her head, arms and legs were missing. Nine-year-old Lucie was the daughter of a cigar-roller, and had last been seen playing with two school friends. She had been accosted by a stranger and given money to buy sweets by the perpetrator, before simply vanishing. Her disappearance and the grisly discovery in the River Spree followed the mutilation of a young woman found dismembered in the Charlottenburg Canal in a sack, and human remains found outside Berlin by travelling showmen. All cases remained unsolved, but whether they were the work of Berger, or related to further cases that materialized in Europe over the next few years was unclear.

Blood Lust

1905

Twenty-two-year-old James Boyne pleaded guilty in May 1905 to a "Jack the Ripper" crime he committed on 3rd April that year. Appearing in court in New York, Boyne explained that he had seen a girl in the street and was "seized" with an uncontrollable desire to maim and kill her. He managed to lure her to a hotel where his behaviour frightened the young woman enough to prompt her to try to escape. He held her captive, but his "bungled" mutilation of the girl gave her time to scream, before she was murdered. She was heard by other guests and Boyne was arrested and charged. Doctors pronounced the murderer, and wannabe ripper killer, a hopeless degenerate and a verdict of murder in the second degree was given. Boyne was incarcerated for life.

"Jack the Ripper" in Germany

1907 and 1909

On 30th July 1907, police were still searching for a man in Berlin who attacked three children within half an hour in the northeast of the city four days before. Each of the young victims was stabbed in the abdomen. On Monday, the same day that the press was full of his heinous attacks on innocent children, the man struck again, and another young child became his fourth victim. One of the earlier victims was able to give police a good description of the man. The unnamed girl told police that the man was not a workman, and slightly built, around 25 years old. He was wearing a well-made checked suit when he carried the child in his arms through the entrance to a tenement house, within a courtyard. Once in the yard, the man carefully laid the child on the ground before deliberately stabbing her. The fourth victim was attacked at 10.30 a.m. The 13-year-old daughter of a butcher was coming down the staircase of an apartment building when the man grasped her from behind. In other reports, another girl – who was 14 – was attacked in the arms and feet as she descended the stairwell of a similar building.

All over the previous weekend, several hundred members of Berlin's huge police force were on duty desperately seeking the attacker. Plain clothes officers were busy scouring the streets across all parts of the city, and parents kept their children indoors.

After examining the victims it was clear that one perpetrator was responsible. Each child had been stabbed with a small, sharp instrument, about two inches in length, which appeared to resemble a shoemaker's awl.

Dubbed "Hans the Ripper", the attacker was back in the press the following day where reports were full of the fourth victim's description of the man who had stabbed her in the Choriner Strasse. Two of the earlier victims were still in hospital, but Marguerite Bravitz died from her injuries. Her body was reported to be lying at her parents' home in the Prenzlan district, and unaccompanied minors were noticeably absent from all parts of Berlin, despite the attacks remaining within the northeast suburbs. No more attacks were made, and Hans evaded the authorities at every turn. For almost two years, Berlin was safe once more for children. But all that changed in 1909.

Panic set in across the city in mid-February that year when a number of women and children were attacked. This time, the ripper had upped the ante. Ten attacks had occurred in broad daylight, in busy quarters, on the 14th and 15th of February, which followed eight earlier ripper attacks. The £50 reward offered for any information leading to the apprehension of the man was increased to £150, while police patrolled the streets day and night. Fran Albertine Henke, a merchant's wife, was attacked by a man with a knife at 10.00 a.m., just a day later, outside a house in the Gitschiner Strasse. She suffered wounds to her left hand and left thigh, before the maniac escaped. An hour later, in the Invaliden Strasse, a 20-year-old girl, who worked in domestic service was attacked by three men, one of whom stabbed her. By 3.00 p.m. that same day, Fran Loobs was attacked in Rixdorf by a man who grabbed her by the throat before stabbing her in the upper part of her thigh. Despite two more knifings, Hans the Ripper evaded capture, and no more reports on the story made it into the public domain. He was never caught. It was never established whether the three men who attacked one of the victims were part of the original attacks in 1907, and no perpetrators were brought to justice.

The Düsseldorf Ripper

1929

Twenty years after the final attacks in Berlin, the body of a young woman was discovered in a field. A letter, sent to the authorities in November 1929 by a "Jack the Ripper"-style killer who had already struck before, gave clues as to where the body could be found. The victim was 20-year-old Maria Hahn, who worked in domestic service and had been missing since 11th August that year. It transpired that Maria had been friends with an earlier victim who was found dead near the Rhine some months before. The young woman had suffered multiple knife wounds. Panic then set in across Germany when an anonymous postcard was received by the *Düsseldorf Mittag* from a man claiming to be the killer. The card said that he would be leaving the area and heading for another (unnamed) town, where it was believed the atrocities would continue.

In mid-November 1929, the police were no further forward in their investigation, but letters of advice were pouring in from across Europe. Meanwhile, all children in Düsseldorf were advised to keep to the main roads and avoid any areas without proper lighting. One of the letters that police received was a grim warning, apparently from the ripper himself. The handwritten note read: "ACHTUNG! POLIZEI ZEIGE WAS DU WERT BIST! FREITAG DEN 22. VORAUSSICHTLICH NACHTER MORD!" – translated it means: "Attention! Police show what you're made of. Friday the 22nd. Expect Murder", according to newspaper reports.

However, no murder took place as far as the police were concerned at the time. In early January 1930, however, a breakthrough was made when one of the ripper's victims recognized her attacker. Frau Meurer, who was seriously injured in October 1929 by the ripper, saw the man who attacked her in Licht Strasse one evening. The woman was paralyzed with fear and couldn't do anything to apprehend the man, who on realizing that the woman in front of him had recognized him, escaped on a passing tram. By the following month, the whole of Düsseldorf was asking whether the German "Jack the Ripper" had been found. In February 1930, a high government official from Bockum, seven miles north of Düsseldorf, was arrested for the attempted murder of a young woman. He remained unnamed while police continued their investigation, but the man's handwriting bore a striking resemblance to that found on the notes that were known to have been written by the murderer. He had written a number of letters to the young woman, who, having seen his handwriting in newspaper articles and noting the similarities, took her letters to the police. She had arranged to meet with the man, and police urged her to keep the date, while they undertook a surveillance operation. While the man and woman met, police spied him putting a white powder in her coffee, which led to his subsequent arrest by detectives. However, two days later, on 8th February 1930, the public believed the Düsseldorf Ripper to be active again when a man, said to resemble the murderer, attempted to kidnap a young child. He had led the child by the hand at least 100 yards, in the hope of boarding a tram, but the child cried out and the mother ran towards the man. He disappeared on the tram leaving the child behind. In March, it was mooted that the killer could be in Holland. A report came in from The Hague of a savage attack on two nurses, one of whom was stabbed to death when they refused to speak to a man they didn't know. He pulled a knife, wounded one nurse who then escaped, while the other suffered a horrific death. The *Mirror* said: "The savage manner of the attack is thought by the police to be identical with that adopted by the 'ripper'".

Two months later, and with 10 victims dead, the police were looking for a link to two more murders that took place at Ratibor in southern Poland. A number of raids took place in the town, and underworld criminals were being watched. However, one gang of eight criminals offered to help police catch the killer and proclaimed that they could track him down in just two weeks. In late May 1930, Peter Kürten was arrested in connection with the Düsseldorf "ripper" murders. Following his remand by police, the Swiss authorities believed that he was also responsible for the death of a 12-year-old girl that took place near Basle. Meanwhile, it was reported that Kürten's trial would be likely to take place at some point in 1931.

In mid-April 1931, Peter Kürten admitted: "I was embittered against humanity". It also transpired at his trial that he had carried scissors in his pocket "to stab someone". Accused of five murders and seven attempted murders, the 48-year-old was placed on trial on 13th April, where he proceeded to tell the shocked courtroom the story of his crimes. With a frightening callousness, Kürten related the details of the horrific crimes that he had admitted to committing. Kürten, the son of a drunken father, said he had often been in prison, where he had suffered from severe punishments. It was this that had turned him against humanity. He remained "wooden" as the indictment was read out. Kürten had been born to working-class parents in Mulheim am Rhein, and was frequently in prison as a youth for theft. His first murder victim was Christine Klein, the nine-year-old daughter of a restaurant owner from his hometown, killed on 25th May 1913. He had intended to steal something from one of the Klein's bedrooms, but in the second room he entered he found the little girl sleeping peacefully. He claimed he would not have killed the child, but he said that the vivid memories of his prison sufferings drove him to it. He was asked by the court president to describe the murders without going into too many "revolting details". Kürten then described assaults on men, women and children, including the attempted murder of 50-year-old Apollonia Kühn, his second victim. He left his home five days after the attack in a foul mood and found Rosa Ohliger crying in a street in Slingern. He stabbed her to death, and the following day returned to where he'd left her corpse intending to burn the body with petrol. He had gazed at Rosa's body for a day, he told the court, before he recounted how he'd killed Maria Hahn and buried her on the Papendall farm. The court adjourned before the killer described killing two girls in one night. Louise Lenzen, 14, and her friend, Gertrude Hamacher, aged six, had met Kürten on a lonely road. He told the younger girl to wait while he took the teenager and slit her throat. He then strangled the younger girl.

He recalled how as a child he had killed animals for the sake of killing. At the age of nine, he had pushed a child off a raft on which they were playing into the Rhine at Mulheim. The boy drowned, while another boy, also playing alongside them, accidently fell into the water and Kürten held him under until he too was dead. At 16, he attempted to strangle a girl. He had an obsession with the chambers of horrors at waxwork exhibitions and even as a youth could see himself as a model in waxwork standing among the noted criminals of the century. It then transpired that Kürten had a wife whom he considered "a wonderful woman", who trusted him and always accepted his explanation of the bloodstains on his clothing following a murder.

Kürten also described himself as a "petty murderer" and claimed that he would have given up individual murders so that he could concentrate on his grand plan, which was to burn, or blow up bridges and large department stores so that he could cause mass panic. Returning to his previous crimes, he admitted to killing Rudolf Scheer, his only male murder victim, simply because no other victims had "crossed his path" that day.

On Saturday 18th April 1931, the number of murders for which Kürten stood trial was raised to 11, including the two playmates he had drowned in the Rhine. He also confessed to drowning a third child in the harbour at Cologne-Mulheim, a suburb of Cologne. However, it was the evidence of Gertrude Schulte, whom he had attempted to murder, that provided the most damning case against Kürten. She had gone to the fair with Kürten – who was routinely unfaithful to his wife – in August 1929. He took her for a walk along the Rhine and attacked her when they sat down. She was left unconscious with stab wounds.

Kürten was found guilty of nine murders and sentenced to death nine times and also received a 15-year prison sentence for seven attempted murders. What would actually happen was uncertain as, in 1931, capital punishment was in abeyance in Germany. In June that same year, Kürten, by now behind bars, was said to be a physical and nervous wreck as he waited to hear his fate. On 2nd July 1931, Peter Kürten faced the guillotine in the yard of the famous State Prison at Cologne. It was reported that he feared his own death greatly.

The Blackheath Ripper

1931

Towards the end of January 1931 it was thought that footprints and marks made by particular types of car would prove valuable clues in the search for the murderer of Louisa Maud Steel, a domestic servant from Plumstead, who was found dead on Blackheath, in London on 23rd January. Her body had been badly mutilated and press reports likened the crime to those of Jack the Ripper. Superintendent Cooper and Chief Constable Ashley, who headed up the investigation, believed that the 19-year-old had been strangled elsewhere before her body was brought to Blackheath by car. She was found by a man named Hall, a lamplighter, who discovered the body while doing his rounds. Another man called Sweet, who worked as a painter, had seen three men standing near the body shortly before, and police were searching for their whereabouts. Louisa was found naked, dumped on Blackheath at 7.30 a.m.

Led by two of Scotland Yard's most famous detectives, the investigation began at local garages to see whether any cars had suffered any damage, or had been "borrowed". The body was meanwhile examined by the Home Office pathologist Sir Bernard Spilsbury and, later that night, police issued the following statement: "At 7.55 last night, the young woman left her address in Lee Road, and went to the library in Blackheath village and should have called at the chemist's shop of Butcher Curnow's in Blackheath village. She did not reach the shop and so far as police are aware was not seen until her body was found. Any person who may have seen her either along or in company with anyone at any time during the evening or night should communicate with the police at New Scotland Yard, or any police station." The police theory at the time was that Louisa had been lured into a car, driven by a man, between the library and the chemist's shop. They ranked the murder as one of the most callous and cruel in the annals of recent crime, and believed it was the work of a maniac. One side of the girl's face had been so badly cut with a razor that she was almost unrecognizable. Various parts of her body bore evidence of "fiendish work" with the same instrument. A woman living in South Row, opposite the crime scene, said that a car remained stationary on a footpath leading across the heath for some time. As inquiries continued, it transpired that another woman was attacked at the bottom of Granville Park, Blackheath, the night before Louisa was murdered. Her assailant had simply been interested in her handbag, but police needed to ascertain if there was a connection between the two cases.

In the three years prior to Louisa's death, the police across Britain had 24 unsolved murders on their files. Beatrice Prendergast had been discovered stabbed to death near the sea front at Brighton in 1930. Carrie Whitehouse was found in a ditch near Cheadle in Cheshire in May 1930 and Agnes Kesson, a waitress, was found in a ditch in Epsom, Surrey, the same year. In 1928, five murders remained unsolved; that number rose by a further 19 in the two years that followed, and the majority of the victims were women. Margery Wren was fatally injured in her sweet shop in Ramsgate in 1930; Evelyn Foster was found dying close to the burned remains of her car on a Northumberland Moor, while Mary Learoyd, a Bradford clerk was found murdered on Ilkley Moor, Yorkshire, in 1929. On 26th January 1931, the BBC broadcast a description of a man with a scar, in connection with the Blackheath murder, and there was growing public concern about the increase in serious crime across the country. Three murders had been committed in January 1931 alone. Many complained that the police were "placidly employed" in enforcing petty restrictions on law-abiding citizens, and the newspapers claimed that as a result, 24 murderers were "at large". There was growing public concern about the future of the Metropolitan Police Force, and many felt that there was something wrong within the "guardians of the peace". However, detectives stated that the restrictions placed on statement-taking were to blame for their impeded investigations.

More than 50 CID officers and police continued in the hunt for Louisa Steel's murderer. The police took statements from all those who had been on Blackheath on the night of the murder and one witness thought that her two daughters had seen a man hiding in a bush. Joyce Chivers had told her mother that she didn't want to go near the pond as she'd seen a man hiding there, but looking all around as if looking for someone. The BBC broadcast: "The police are very anxious to trace a young man and a young woman who were seen sitting on a seat at Blackheath ... between 8.00pm and

9.00pm". The girl had been crying, and she named the man as Jack. It was hoped that the young couple might be able to shed light on other people around that night. The case was also the first time in history that police used cinemas to appeal for witnesses. All "picture houses" in the district displayed a photograph of Louisa, alongside a message asking that anyone who had seen her in the company of a man should pass the information to police. The search for the murderer, however, continued to frustrate the investigation. Meanwhile, a woman's bloodstained garment was found at a railway line near Catford, where a man with stained hands was seen at a coffee stall. Blackheath was linked directly by rail and bus to Catford. It was also suggested that the Princess of Wales pond would be dragged. It was just 200 yards from the scene of the crime, while it transpired that the girl seen sobbing close by, as broadcast by the BBC, matched the description of Louisa. The young victim was buried on 29th January 1931 at Plumstead Cemetery.

"IS HE THE RIPPER MURDERER?" read the headline in the *Mirror* on 31st January, as police continued their search for a man with a silent tread. Following certain information received the day before, Scotland Yard detectives made inquiries in the Fulham area of London. It was possible that the murderer of Louisa Steel had attacked two other women earlier that same night, one in Granville Park, the other in Manor Park, Lee, Southeast London. Police did not believe that the motive for the attacks was robbery and both had been grabbed by the throat. The women gave the same description of the man, who was said to be 5ft 8in tall, aged between 25 and

35, wearing a dark coat and dark cap, pulled well down over his eyes. He had a peculiar slouching gait and an almost silent tread. To allay the fears of Blackheath residents, the police had drafted in more officers to the area, and a number of women officers were allotted to the district so that women would feel they had female support, and people to talk to. However, people were asking if the murderer would evade capture. Louisa Steel's movements the night she died were still unknown, and women remained fearful of further attacks. The police launched a new appeal on 5th February.

On 17th February 1931, John George Pilgrim, an unemployed youth of 19, appeared at Nottingham on the charge of attempting to murder Josephine Ada Mary Payne, 23, with whom he was having a relationship. It was stated that the couple walked into a house near the canal, and the girl had injuries to her throat. Superintendent Doubleday said that Pilgrim was found to have newspaper cuttings about the Blackheath murder when he was apprehended. He was remanded. On the same day, "Murder against some person or persons unknown", was the verdict at the inquest in Greenwich on Louisa Steel. Sir Bernard Spilsbury described the result of the examination of the body. The girl's black cotton dress had a tape half an inch wide sewn around the upper edge of the neck. The cause of death was asphyxia due to strangulation, by something pressed around the front and side of the neck. The depression on the victim's neck corresponded fairly closely with the tape on the neck of the dress. Spilsbury was fairly confident that Louisa had been attacked from behind and her dress drawn forcibly backwards while counter pressure was applied to the back of the head and neck. The pressure would have been too much for the young woman to cry out and she probably lost consciousness. The pathologist also stated for the inquest that Louisa had lived for some time after her virtual strangulation. She was then subjected to mutilation while still alive. However, the wounds to her chest had occurred post-mortem, he said. He also felt that rather than being strangled and moved, that Louisa had been attacked on the spot where she died on the heath. Inspector Cory told the inquiry that Louisa had been a girl of "high character, and good moral habits". She was not known to have any male friends, or "undesirable acquaintances", and when asked, the inspector said in his opinion that Louisa Steel had been attacked by a "maniac – an insane person".

On 25th February, after being sentenced at Barnet to six months imprisonment, a man made a statement to the police declaring that he had been responsible for the murder of Louisa, but the police attached no importance to the confession. Fresh inquiries made by Scotland Yard some six months later failed to provide the police with anything new to go on. Then, in December 1931, the body of 10-year-old Vera Page from Notting Hilll was found almost covered by earth in the front garden of a house in Addison Road, Kensington. Police immediately began scouring the whole of London for a young man driving a saloon. It was believed that Vera was abducted in a car and murdered in a house or shed. She had been assaulted and strangled before being discovered by a milkman making his early morning rounds. She had also suffered from terrible head injuries.

A man in the Notting Hill area of London had been operating for a week, stopping children and offering them toys and sweets before luring them into his car. Vera had arrived home from school but run to her aunt's house to collect some swimming certificates that she had been awarded. However, she was known to be shy of strangers. The little girl had been seen chatting to a man who matched the description of the Blackheath ripper shortly before she disappeared, and everything about the crime scene, reported the *Mirror*, seemed "to point to the work of a maniac, such as the man who attacked and killed Louisa Steel on Blackheath some months ago." However, there was no further evidence to link the two deaths and nothing was ever proved against any perpetrator, although rumours with regard to the man's identity were rife. What was clear, however, was that Louisa Steel had been murdered in a similar manner to the women of Victorian Whitechapel some 40 years or so before. Nothing like it had been seen since the time of Jack the Ripper, but the mutilations were typical of a crazed ripper killer. Louisa had been gagged following strangulation before she suffered terrible mutilation while still alive. A man driving a small saloon car, like the one seen when Vera was abducted, was known to have spoken to a number of women that night on the pretence of asking directions. The case was never solved.

Death Threats

1931

"You die at twelve to-morrow mid-night-Ripper", read the threatening notes, which were pushed through the letterboxes of two Chippenham residents in mid-February 1931. At the time, the murder of Louisa Steel was still undergoing investigation and people were scared. And a third note, signed "Ripper", was placed in one of the town's pillar-boxes. One of the two residents who received the threatening note was subsequently attacked under a dark railway arch when returning home at night from his job as a clerk. The whole town was extremely worried by the anonymous threats made by someone calling themselves a ripper. Nineteen-year-old George Gale was the clerk from Lowden, on the outskirts of Chippenham, who received the note that said on the other side: "My thirst for blood.-Ripper" and a drawing of a sabre. At first, despite simultaneous knocking on the back and front door, and the note in the letterbox, George Gale treated the matter as a joke, until he was attacked the following night. A man grabbed the young man and shone a torch in his face telling him that if he valued his life he'd watch his step. He was then kneed in the back and sent sprawling. When he got up, the man was running away towards the town centre. Another resident of Lowden, a middle-aged man living about a quarter of a mile away from George Gale, also received a note through his letterbox. The third note read: "J. Ripper will be on the bridge to-morrow at 3.30am". Apart from the attack on George, there were no more "ripper" incidents in Chippenham.

The Blackout Ripper

1942

Police investigated two murders in early February 1942. The first victim was a woman found strangled in a London air raid shelter. The other woman was found in Victoria Park, Southport, Lancashire, and identified as 28-year-old Maria Osliff, a nurse. A day later, the electricity meter man called at a first-floor room in Wardour Street, Soho, London, on 2nd February 1942. There was no answer to his repeated knocking, so he and a woman neighbour pushed the door open. They saw Nita Ward lying across the bed. She was wearing nothing but a short jacket and what seemed to be a red scarf around her neck. But, it wasn't a red scarf. Nita Ward had been brutally murdered and her throat cut by a tin opener that was found bloodstained in the room with the murder victim. The 32-year-old (real name Mrs Evelyn Oatley), was fascinated by life in the West End of London. On the Monday night before Nita was found, her radio had been blaring out and disturbing many of her neighbours, who now wondered if it had been put on deliberately to drown the sound of her cries. Divisional Detective Inspector Gray, from C Division was put in charge of the case and immediately ordered his men to begin taking statements from people in Soho clubs. The police now had three murdered women in two days to investigate. The woman found in the air raid shelter was identified as Mrs Evelyn

Margaret Hamilton, 35, a chemist from Hornchurch in Essex, who had recently quit her job and her room, telling her landlady that she was moving to Grimsby. The next victim to be found was Mrs Susan Wilkinson, 43, who had her head battered in a lonely lane near her home. Police were alerted by her husband who became alarmed when his wife did not return home after a visit to a doctor's house. Another woman had been attacked in the same lane a week before, but she screamed out and her attacker fled the scene. By 14th February, two more women were dead, found strangled in the West End of London. Mrs Margaret Lawe, 45, was found in a flat in Gosfield Street, West London. The week before she had been assaulted by a Canadian soldier but refused to bring charges. An hour after her body was found, Mrs Doris Jouannet, 32, wife of a hotel manager, was found at a flat in Sussex Gardens, not far away.

On 17th February a man was charged at Bow Street in London with the murders of Doris, Margaret and Evelyn (Nita). He was named as RAF leading aircraftman Gordon Frederick Cummins, 28, who was remanded. However, a fresh jury had to be called in April 1942 when a document was handed to the jury by mistake. It was thought that it could prejudice the case. Dubbed by the press as the "most notorious killer since Jack the Ripper", newspaper headlines read: "Ripper Gets Sentence of Death", on 29th April. He was sentenced to death at the gallows at the Old Bailey, where the jury heard how, according to Mr Justin Asquith, he had killed Nita Ward in a "sadistic sexual murder of a ghoulish type". Cummins had used a safety razor blade to hack at her throat until she was virtually dead, and while she lay dying and gasping for her last breaths, he used a tin opener to gash and mutilate her.

The murders by Cummins had given Scotland Yard its biggest murder hunt in more than 50 years. Women decoys had been employed to "trap" the ripper killer, but on 13th February, the murderer had given up his identity when he tried to claim another victim, Greta Heywood, in a Haymarket air raid shelter. As the woman screamed, he left behind his gas mask, with his name and service number. Mrs Heywood ran to a police station and the respirator was soon found. That wasn't all he left behind. Cummins' fingerprints were found on a mirror in Nita Ward's room, as well as the tin opener. Newspapers dubbed Cummins a "modern ripper". He was executed at Wandsworth Prison in London on 25th June 1942.

Robert Whalley

1966

In August 1966 a "laughing killer", who boasted that he had already stabbed two people to death, left a note on the doorstep of a police headquarters saying that he would claim a third victim – a teenager. Detectives believed the killer and said: "We are searching for a dangerous killer, a maniac." With the note in a parcel found outside the main police station in Stockport, Cheshire, was a dagger with its tip missing. Police scientists decided that the dagger was the one plunged into the back of John Crossland, 44, of Cheadle Heath, who had been found dying of stab wounds a few days before. The broken dagger blade fitted perfectly to an inch-long dagger tip found in Crossland's body. Two pieces of crumpled paper with words cut from newspaper headlines made up the note. Crossland was named in the note, along with Mrs Marjorie Hill, 42, from Hazel Grove, who was stabbed to death the year before. The end of the note said: "My next victim will be a teenager ... ha ha", crying echoes of the words used by Jack the Ripper, who frequently wrote "ha ha" in letters to the police. Detective Chief Superintendent Cyril Wilkes said: "We fully believe this man will strike again ... He has identified himself with the knife." Police called the man the "laughing killer" because as he left Marjorie dying, there was a burst of laughter. Mrs Hill and Mr Crossland died at spots little more than two and a half miles from each other – in lonely, dark areas frequented by courting couples and peeping toms. Wilkes added: "I want all teenagers to heed my warning to be on the alert. They are in danger. It is impossible at this stage to know where this killer will strike again. This man may be on the face of it, a perfectly normal individual – perhaps a father of children. But he may show signs of mental stress which only his family know about." The newspaper letters used in the note were taken from the *Mirror* distributed in northern editions. This provided police with vital information.

On Friday 19th August 1966, a crowd of 300 screaming people tried to attack a man charged with the two murders. Robert Leonard Whalley, 24, was guarded by 30 policemen as he was escorted from a court at Stockport where he had been remanded. As they tried to reach Whalley, the crowd punched and kicked at the policemen. One woman aimed a blow with her handbag at Whalley whose head was covered by a coat. A man punched him on the back and police had to force a path through jeering people before they could put the accused in a car. Then the angry crowd which jammed Warren Street in Stockport launched an attack on the car. They kicked and slapped it as it was slowly driven away. A policeman who was punched on the jaw said afterwards: "I never want to face a mob like that again." Even the magistrate had to fight his way through the crowd to reach the court building. In a six-minute court appearance, Whalley, a coal merchant's assistant from Cheadle Heath, was charged with the murder of both Mrs Hill and Mr Crossland. It was reported that he had told police he was guilty.

When Whalley's trial began, Timothy Taylor, prosecuting, told the court that the accused had a "lust for killing", and had tried to imitate Jack the Ripper. Marjorie Hill, a mother of four, was stabbed in a field in Bramhall, Cheshire, in August 1966. The following August, John Crossland died after being knifed in a wood in Cheadle, Cheshire. Whalley had, by this time, made a statement which was virtually a confession to the crimes. He even took police to several spots where knives were recovered, including the weapon used to kill Mrs Hill. In the coalman's home in Sherborne Road, Cheadle Heath, more knives were found, along with a number of books on Jack the Ripper.

Robert Whalley was sent to Broadmoor in December 1966, but was found dead in July the following year. He'd been described at his trial as a very dangerous man, who committed murder on nothing but impulse.

Peter Sutcliffe – The Yorkshire Ripper

1975

On 10th July 1977, a woman believed to be the latest victim of the Yorkshire Ripper was lying gravely injured in hospital. Detectives waited by the bed of 42-year-old Maureen Long, who was found with serious head and body injuries early that day on waste ground in Laister Dyke, Bradford, West Yorkshire. She was still wearing the long black evening gown in which she had danced the night away at Bradford's Bali Hai dancehall. Police believed that she was attacked soon after leaving, and that the attacker could be the man who had murdered five times in the previous 20 months. Four of his victims were sex workers, which brought comparisons with Jack the Ripper. George Oldfield, Assistant Chief Constable of West Yorkshire, who headed the hunt for the Ripper, rushed to Bradford to take charge of the investigation.

He said: "Mrs. Long has already been able to give us a little assistance. The possibility she could have been attacked by the man we are already seeking is uppermost in my mind." The victim, who was separated from her husband, was known to enjoy going out to dance and socialize.

Three schoolgirls fought off a sex fiend who could have been the

Yorkshire Ripper in early October 1977. The desperate struggle took place less than half a mile from the spot where Carol Wilkinson, 20, was savagely beaten just 24 hours earlier. She almost lost her life. A man in blue jeans grabbed a 12-year-old on the Ravenscliffe Estate in Bradford, but her two school friends rushed to her rescue and fought with the man, who ran away. A police spokesman said: "These youngsters were very courageous – when this man took hold of one of them the others didn't run away, but went for him instead." Carol, meanwhile, was critically ill in hospital, after being kept alive by a life-support machine at Bradford Royal Infirmary. She had been found lying in a pool of blood after being bludgeoned and sexually assaulted near her home. Police believed her attacker was the same person who had killed Mary Gregson, 38, in Shipley, six weeks earlier. Over the previous two years, five women had been killed between Leeds and Bradford in a series of "Jack the Ripper"-style murders. Detectives hunting the sex attacker warned Bradford's women and children not to go out alone.

A helicopter was called in to aid the search for the man the three girls described as bearded, in his twenties, and dressed in denim. There were fears that the Ripper had crossed the Pennines to Manchester too, as detectives probed a "nude in the hedge" murder riddle. The victim, they believed, had been attacked by the Ripper. The latest victim, police thought, was a 20-year-old mother who vanished from her home 11 days earlier. She was found savagely battered on the head and body just a mile from where she lived in Manchester's Moss Side. Detectives believed that she could have lain dead, behind an allotment hedge, since she disappeared on 1st October 1977. Detective Chief Superintendent Jack Ridgeway, heading the hunt for the killer, said: "We're fairly certain we have identified the woman." Meanwhile, the costs of the case continued to rise and in November that year had passed the £1 million mark. It was still rising, however, as the bid to capture the six-times killer entered its third year. Detectives in West Yorkshire had spent a total of 425,000 hours on the manhunt, and officers in Greater Manchester were also involved, when it was proved that the missing mother, eventually named as 21-year-old Jean Royle, was a ripper victim. Police forces throughout the country had had to trace more than 120,000 drivers. Some of the detectives on the case had been working on it for more than two years and had interviewed nearly 200,000 people. But, in November 1977, they had to begin again, with an endless task of ploughing through the mountain of information in the murder HQ at Millgarth police station in Leeds. "We are checking every detail on all our murders yet again," confirmed George Oldfield. "We may not have appreciated the significance of some tiny clue before and we hope it will emerge this time." His murder squad had, at times, been 300-strong, but by the end of 1977, just 40 officers were engaged full time on the inquiry.

It had begun with the murder of mother of four Wilma McCann in October 1975. In the months that followed, the Ripper attacked at least five more women in Leeds and Bradford, and one of the victims survived her atrocious attack. One of the problems that the team faced was frustration at the ongoing lack of success. However, the job had to go on before the killer struck again. As Detective Chief Inspector Len Bradley put it: "This is why a full team is being kept so active on this hunt." Police had amassed a huge amount of information about the murders, and more than 71,000 clues had been followed up, 45,000 checks had been made on car tyres, and nearly 10,000 statements had been taken. The most vital lead was a £5 note found in the handbag of victim, Jean Royle. Police strongly suspected that the man they were looking for was employed in the Bradford–Shipley area.

Just a few months later, in March 1978, it was suggested that a second ripper could be on the prowl in Yorkshire. Police feared that he may be a copycat killer, jealous of the Ripper's notoriety, and determined to outscore him. The rival ripper, it was believed, could have butchered three women to death. The chilling suspicions came about when it was shown that sex worker Yvonne Pearson was not the Ripper's eighth victim. The mutilated body of the 22-year-old mother was found on a derelict site in the heart of Bradford's red-light district. At first it was thought she was the Ripper's victim – by now his tally had reached the killings and mutilation of six sex workers and a 16-year-old girl in the previous three years – but a pathologist told the police that her injuries were unlike those common to the Yorkshire Ripper's MO. However, they were similar, though "much more horrific". It was hoped that Yvonne's secret address book would trap her killer and the Yorkshire Ripper. In the book, the young woman named 46 regular customers, which she kept hidden in her home. Many names in the book were clients outside Yorkshire, and detectives thought the Ripper could be travelling in to Leeds and Bradford to pick up his victims. Her book came as a surprise to her friends and acquaintances, including a fellow sex worker who didn't know of any other woman who kept one. All her clients, from Yorkshire, the Midlands and Leicester were traced by police and Detective Superintendent Trevor Lapish, of West Yorkshire Police said: "It might be in their own interest if men who knew Yvonne came forward of their own accord … otherwise they face the embarrassment of police officers knocking on their door."

A girl found murdered on 5th August 1979 was thought to be the Ripper's 11th victim. Detectives probing the brutal killing of 19-year-old Josephine Whitaker investigated a possible link with the Ripper's trail of horror. Up to this time, he had killed 10 women in three and a half years. Josephine was a Halifax Building Society clerk who was savagely attacked just before midnight as she walked home across playing fields after visiting her grandmother. She was believed to have died almost immediately, but six hours went by before a woman on her way to work discovered the body in Savile Park, Halifax, just a few hundred yards from her home. Josephine had head injuries and wounds to other parts of her body. Of the other victims, three had died in Leeds, two in Bradford, one in Manchester, one in Huddersfield and one in Preston. The "Ripper" squad joined other detectives in the hunt for Josephine's killer. Home Office pathologist Professor David Gee, who had examined all the Ripper victims, was called in to carry out a post-mortem on the young woman. Both Ridgeway and Oldfield were called to urgent meetings. It was not unusual for Josephine to visit her grandmother on Huddersfield Road and to walk home to where she lived with her parents and two younger brothers. The night she was brutally murdered, she had decided to walk home, despite the late hour, because she needed to put her contact lenses in their pot overnight and she had work the next day. There were a few people about, mainly walking dogs, so it was Josephine that the Ripper targeted when he saw her walking alone. He knew she wasn't a prostitute, but by that time he needed to kill. He talked to the young girl as she walked. She told him that she rode horses, that she'd been to see her grandmother and that she was on her way home. She told him it was quite a walk, and that she often took a short cut across the field. Ironically, Sutcliffe later stated that he told Josephine that you didn't know who you could trust. He asked Josephine the time and she looked at the clock tower. He then remarked on how good her eyesight was and pretended to linger, peering at the clock as he drew his hammer from inside his coat. He hit Josephine on the back of the head and she fell to the ground, moaning loudly. She was still moaning as the Ripper hit her again. But he then panicked when he noticed two people walking nearby. He dragged the young victim by her ankles away from the road (which was close by), with her face in the dirt before he found a "safe" spot away from unsuspecting passers-by. He turned Josephine over, removed some of her clothes and began mutilating her body in a frenzied attack. With his senses heightened, the Ripper worked quickly, aware that people were not far away. He left Josephine to die from her head and stabbing injuries with her coat covering the main part of her body. The next morning as a flurry of activity surrounded the crime scene, Josephine's 13-year-old brother was walking close to the park when he saw police surrounding something on the ground. He immediately recognized his sister's shoe, lying on the ground, and ran home to tell his mother and stepfather. They immediately called the police as the horror of what had happened began to unfold.

"Phone clue in Ripper hunt", read the headlines on 10th April 1979. A mystery phone caller, it was alleged, could hold the secret to the Yorkshire Ripper. The caller gave police vital information in their hunt for the crazed killer, but he rang off before he could be persuaded to give his name. The man leading the hunt, George Oldfield, urged the caller to come forward. The man had phoned police in Halifax with information about a Datsun car, which was seen near the spot where Josephine Whitaker was murdered the week before. Police also issued a photofit of the man they wanted to interview. He had been seen driving a Ford Escort in the town centre and was described as scruffy and of average build. The photofit didn't show a bearded man, but it showed a dark-haired man with a moustache. It wasn't completely removed from the man they desperately needed to find. On 17th April, hundreds of firms were urged to help in the hunt for the ripper killer. The move came after detectives built up a detailed description of the man responsible for the murder of 11 women. They were convinced that he was an engineer who lived in Yorkshire and had some connection with

Tyneside. George Oldfield said: "I want to know if any engineering firm in Yorkshire had a man working in the North East on March 7th and 8th, March 12th and 13th, and March 22nd and 23rd. I believe the man is white, aged 30 to 55, living or working in or near West Yorkshire." He thought that the Ripper lived alone, or with aged parents, and that he was skilled, or semi-skilled, as a machine-tool fitter or an electrical or maintenance engineer. Then, on 25th June, it was reported that the voice of the man who claimed to be the Yorkshire Ripper could be broadcast to the nation. Detectives were expected to make a tape public that had been sent to them the week before. On the recording, the man said that he was the killer, and police hoped that the public could help them identify him.

Two of the victims who survived relived their terrifying ordeal in a bid to trap the killer when they listened to the tape recording of the man claiming to be the Ripper. The man had a gruff Geordie accent, and threatened to claim a further victim in Manchester. Maureen Long had talked with the Ripper briefly as he drove her to a lonely spot before attacking her. The recording was eventually broadcast on 26th June 1979. It resulted in a barrage of calls to police after it went out on TV and radio. More than 100 people rang police in Greater Manchester claiming they could help. Sex workers, among whom the voice on the recording said he would claim his next victim, were warned by the police to be vigilant. Two days later, more than 1,000 men waited for police to knock on their door uttering the words: "Someone believes you are the Yorkshire Ripper." The massive dragnet followed the broadcast where the man taunted police for failing to catch him. He also vowed that the slaughter of innocent women would continue. All calls made to police were carefully checked, and George Oldfield challenged the Ripper to meet him. Offering to arrange a rendezvous any time, any place, Mr Oldfield said: "He has caused enough grief already. In his own interest he should give himself up." Meanwhile, a handwriting expert, Diane Simpson, called in by police to study letters that could have been sent by the Ripper, said: "The writer is clearly highly dangerous." She explained that the writing revealed violent characteristics – and that the writer had an engineering or mechanical background. But questions still riddled the Ripper "Dossier". The biggest was why he struck at random times. Only a few weeks separated some killings, but twice he had gone 12 months before he struck again. Was he working out of the country? Was he in prison? Was he a voluntary mental patient? Why were all three letters and the tape recording posted in Tyne and Wear? Was he a worker whose job took him there, or did he visit friends? Why did the Ripper mostly kill along the length of the trans-Pennine motorway? Was he a religious crank? Or was he impotent? Why did he pick on sex workers in the main? There were as many theories as there were psychiatrists, but there weren't that many facts. Even forensic scientists were surprised by the lack of evidence after four years and 15 attacks.

The Yorkshire Ripper had shown amazing cunning – or knowledge – to avoid leaving clues after the murders. But some evidence had been pieced together. The murder weapon hadn't been found by mid-1979, but from the victim's injuries, it was believed he worked in engineering and killed with a tool from his workbench. A footprint had been found close to the body of one of the dead women and suggested the attacker was wearing heavy industrial boots. The £5 note, found in a hidden folder in Jean Royle's purse when she was found dead, was one of a batch of £25,000 issued to Yorkshire works four days before her death, and the tyre marks showed the killer drove an old banger with worn tyres. The three letters had been carefully handled so as to avoid any marks on them, while the tape recording gave details of the killings that the police had kept quiet.

Several psychiatrists constructed profiles of the Ripper, since he was identified as a serial, ripper killer. The psychiatrist who made the closest study of him was Dr Stephen Shaw, a consultant at Stanley Royd Hospital in Wakefield. He believed that the Ripper was an "over controlled, aggressive psychopath", meaning that most of the time he bottled up his emotions far beyond the point at which a normal man would explode with anger. Dr Shaw stated: "In his everyday life he appears to be a man completely in control of himself ... the tensions that build up inside him could be totally unrecognised by family or friends."

"He's a real life Jekyll and Hyde," said police spokesman Graham King. "The pressure builds up until something breaks inside him. Then he goes out and murders as a form of relief. Afterwards he goes home again quite normally." It was also suggested that the Ripper was a schizophrenic, but as he'd written to police and sent a tape recording it seemed unlikely according to experts. It was suggested that what family and friends might notice is that just prior to killing, the man suffered from headaches and irritability due to the tension and turmoil building up inside him.

Many comparisons were made between Jack the Ripper and the Yorkshire Ripper, which included the fact that both killed at night. Both targeted sex workers, and mutilation was horrifically inflicted on the victims. Both rippers were capable of disappearing without trace, and neither seemed concerned at the huge numbers of police deployed to hunt them down. Jack the Ripper was suspected of taunting police with his letters, while the Yorkshire Ripper was supposed to have sent the note that read: "I see you are still having no luck catching me ... I'm not quite sure where I'll strike again but it will be definitely this year. THE YORKSHIRE RIPPER 1979."

At the end of June 1979, the *Mirror* told the story of Olive Smelt. Alasdair Buchan wrote: "Death walked up to Olive Smelt one evening four years ago, commented pleasantly on the weather, then tried to end her life in a most brutal fashion." Olive was battered to the ground, her skull dented in several places with a blunt weapon, her face was cut and her attacker took the first gruesome steps to cutting her body open. "But death was cheated," continued Buchan. "Young lovers switched on their car headlights at the far end of a dark, narrow Halifax street and unwittingly came to Olive's rescue." Olive wasn't a sex worker, she was a housewife of 46, who survived her horrific ordeal. Only three other women had seen the face of the Ripper and lived to tell the tale. The *Mirror* reported that four years after the attack, Olive occasionally forced herself to walk along the street where it happened. She told Buchan: "I don't want to spend the rest of my life hiding away. The last thing I remember was this man, in his early thirties, coming up to me in the street and saying that the weather was getting better."

Olive was attacked just before midnight and was walking home after visiting friends. She was just a few yards from the safety of her front door. "He wasn't very frightening," she recalled. "He was less than six feet and he didn't look all that strong. He walked on and suddenly I was struck from behind. I don't remember anything until I woke up in hospital." The police believed they knew the weapon used by the Ripper, but they were keeping the details confidential for fear of copycat assaults. A special mark – the Ripper's trademark – was scored on Olive's body, but that too was kept private. What the car headlights did was save Olive from being ripped open and her entrails being pulled out. It was believed that while his victims were not sexually assaulted, the Ripper was getting his sexual kicks from what he was doing.

Meanwhile, each of the four photofit images of the Ripper were withdrawn. "There has never been a killer like him before in Britain," wrote the *Mirror* at the end of June 1979. "The Yorkshire Ripper has committed more murders than Jack the Ripper ... he killed 11 with a brutality that made even hardened murder squad men still the chat with which they make their work bearable." All but one of his victims was linked by the motorway network which sliced 50 miles across the Pennines from Leeds to Manchester. The other victim was murdered in Preston, 30 miles up the M61 from Manchester. Each victim was obscenely mutilated.

George Oldfield continued to listen impassively to the tape that the "Ripper" had sent him. The voice he listened to was calm, so calm that it was frightening. The tape was three minutes long and sounded as though it was made in a small room by one man. There are pauses throughout, interspersed with a Geordie voice making jibes and boasts. By now the costs of hunting him down had exceeded £3 million – at the time, the most expensive manhunt Britain had ever seen. Yet, the police were desperate and needed more help from the public. The sex workers of Leeds had been more careful for a time, but they didn't want to speak to the police much. Some women teamed up and one took down car registrations while the other left with the punter, but even that didn't last long. After a year of no Ripper activity in Leeds – his favoured hunting ground – even that small insurance waned. In a letter, the Ripper told police how he wouldn't be back in Chapeltown, the red-light district of Leeds: "Too bloody hot there." But, he'd been known to strike in Manningham, one of Bradford's twilight areas. He'd also written to the *Mirror*, who handed the letter to police. The *Mirror* also suggested that the chilling tape recording was released on an answering machine, so that anyone could call the number and listen to the voice. It was hoped that someone, somewhere would recognize it.

In a move to trap the Ripper, police announced that they would be visiting every home in Sunderland – where experts believed the man on the tape came from. On 3rd September 1979, it was feared he'd struck again when the badly mutilated body of a young woman was found in the centre of Bradford. The gruesome find was made by a police officer, and a Home Office pathologist was called to compare the horrific injuries suffered by the woman to the Ripper's "trademarks". Police had spent many man hours by this time trawling Wearside in Tyne and Wear to track the man on the tape. The latest victim was found at the rear of a mid-Victorian terraced house, while Jack Ridgeway, by now investigating two Ripper attacks in Manchester, rushed to the murder scene. The new victim, whom it was established was killed by the Ripper, was a student. Babs Leach made the fatal mistake of walking home alone from a late-night party. Within minutes of leaving her friends, she was dead. She became the 12th victim of a madman.

Babs, 20, was killed within 500 yards of Bradford's police HQ among the lights, music and late-night wanderers in the city's university bedsit area. Detectives believed that the Ripper checked the area again and again as he waited for September and the first intake of students to return to the city after the summer holidays. Babs, from Kettering in Northamptonshire, had decided to leave her flatmates to walk alone after a Saturday night pub party. Wearing a cotton shirt and jeans, she'd walked just 200 yards before the Ripper struck. He knocked her unconscious then dragged her down an unlit alleyway into the backyard of no. 13 Ashgrove. There he killed and mutilated her, concealing the body under a pile of rubbish. No one saw or heard anything. Her killer got a 39-hour head start before a policeman found her body. The Ripper had chillingly said he would probably kill in September, in Bradford. Babs had returned to Bradford to begin her third year at university studying social sciences. She was a keen rider, fond of animals, and had two cats and a dog. Her parents travelled from Kettering to identify her body. Less than two months later, on 4th November, a man claiming to be the Yorkshire Ripper phoned the *Daily Mirror* with a "terrifying message". He warned police that he would kill again within the coming weeks. His eight-minute call was listened to by police, who firmly believed he could be the Ripper, and it was reported that the call and the tape would be analyzed and compared. The man in the recording said: "I intend to keep going for quite a while yet. I'll chop myself up rather than get caught. But I'm warning you that I will be striking again within the next few weeks – may be in Warrington, Wigan or Widnes. I like it in the North. There's plenty of them knocking about there." The man, who kept putting coins in the box, told the *Mirror* switchboard operator who taped the call: "It's no good looking for fingerprints. I'll be away from this phone box by the time you have taped this call." Two weeks later, the Ripper wrote a remorseful letter saying he was sorry for the murder of 16-year-old Jayne MacDonald, his sixth victim. The shop assistant had died when she took a shortcut home through Chapeltown in Leeds. Part of the letter read: "About the MacDonald lassie I didn't know that she was decent and I am sorry I changed my routine that night." Jayne's mother responded to the letter by saying: "What was the use of saying sorry. You can't bring her back." Mrs Irene MacDonald had had two tragedies to cope with brought about by the Ripper. After her daughter was murdered, Mrs MacDonald's husband, Wilf, never recovered from their loss and died of a broken heart.

In late November 1979, it was announced that tax officials had refused to open their files to detectives hunting the Ripper. Police wanted to compare samples of the killer's handwriting with entries on tax returns, but the Inland Revenue – as it was then – stuck strictly to the rules and a spokesman said: "All tax records are confidential." However, the Department of Health and Social Security did help the police and several local offices opened their files for handwriting checks. A day later, on 21st November, it was reported that two top Scotland Yard detectives were to join the hunt. West Yorkshire police had said they didn't need the Yard, but after four years and 12 murders they changed their minds. Commander James Nevill, former head of the Anti-Terrorist Squad, and Detective Chief Superintendent Joseph Bolton, travelled from London to Leeds, where they were to look at police strategy, the lines of inquiry and the deployment of personnel.

In February 1980, police wondered if the Ripper had killed himself and made inquiries about suicide victims, because they couldn't discount the possibility that the man would take his own life if things became too hot. The Ripper's 13th victim, however, was killed on 17th November 1980. Jackie Hill, a 20-year-old student, was believed to have met her killer on a bus as she took the two-mile ride home from Cookridge Street in Leeds to Headingley. Minutes after she got off the bus, along with five other passengers, she was brutally murdered.

By the end of the month women's groups were up in arms over the police's failure to capture the Ripper, demanding that women be allowed to carry weapons to protect themselves, while MPs called for Scotland Yard to take over the five-year hunt. A new team, headed by Detective Chief Superintendent James Hobson, was implemented following mounting criticism of police methods and the censure of three officers over the mishandling of a vital clue – a bloodstained handbag which they mistakenly logged as lost property – in the killing of Jackie Hill. Other members of the team included Commander Ronald Harvey, West Midlands Assistant Chief Constable David Gerty, Thames Valley Deputy Chief Constable Leslie Emment, Home Office forensic expert Stuart Kind and Lincolnshire Assistant Chief Constable Andrew Sloan.

On 27th November 1980, a TV message aimed at one viewer, the Yorkshire Ripper, was aired containing messages from the relatives of some of his victims and two women who survived his crazed attacks. In the programme, he was described as "an evil, sexually-inadequate coward". The seven-minute recording was part of the BBC's *Newsnight* programme. It was a powerful item, followed by West Yorkshire police urging people to come forward to help them find the Ripper. Mothers, fathers, an aunt, and two women who were attacked spoke with hate and bitterness. They belittled the Ripper, and many called him a coward. They also spoke directly to the woman who police believed was harbouring the Ripper. They appealed to her moral sensibilities to come forward and give up the man who had brought such feelings of hatred to West Yorkshire and beyond.

Meanwhile, unemployed labourer, Steven Bainbridge, 24, of

Fleetwood, Lancashire, who phoned the *Mirror* saying he was the Ripper, was imprisoned in November 1980 for three months after admitting making a threat to kill. Elsewhere, prisoners at four of Britain's prisons called for their friends in the underworld to join forces with the police and catch the Ripper. The police welcomed the offer.

But the biggest breakthrough was to come in January 1981. A man, arrested on Friday 2nd January, was held for questioning by police and appeared in court three days later. The man, in his thirties, was in a parked car with a sex worker when he was arrested. He was spotted by two officers on patrol in the red-light district of Sheffield, who suspected that the number plates on the Rover V8 were false. The uniformed officers moved in to question the driver, who was in the woman's arms. Dissatisfied with the answers they received, the police arrested the driver and he was taken to Dewsbury for questioning by senior detectives. West Yorkshire's Chief Constable Ronald Gregory told reporters that the man could face a serious charge, although he wouldn't say what. He also said: "We are absolutely delighted with the developments at this stage." The man's house in Bradford was under police guard.

Sergeant Robert Ring and Constable Robert Hydes saw the car with what appeared to be false plates in Havelock Square in Sheffield. The driver was with a local vice girl, who was known to police. He was booked for a traffic offence, but after several hours of questioning, a message was flashed to the Ripper squad who raced to Sheffield and took him to Dewsbury. Despite no longer heading the investigation following a heart attack brought about by his dedication of bringing the Ripper to justice, George Oldfield told reporters: "It is confirmed that a man arrested in Sheffield in connection with another matter is being questioned by West Yorkshire police officers in connection with the Yorkshire Ripper inquiry." The victims who died included: Wilma McCann, 28, Joan Harrison, 26, Emily Jackson, 42, Irene Richardson, 28, Patricia Atkinson, 33, Jayne MacDonard, 16, Jean Jordan, 21, Yvonne Pearson, 22, Helen Rytka, 18, Vera Millward, 41, Josephine Whitaker, 19, Barbara (Babs) Leach, 20 and Jacqueline Hill, 20. Of the four women who survived, it was hoped that they would identify the man now in custody.

On 6th January 1981, Peter Sutcliffe arrived at a Yorkshire court to face a charge of murdering 20-year-old student Jacqueline Hill. More than 1,000 people gathered outside the courthouse in Dewsbury, ready for the arrival of a three-vehicle police convoy. Sutcliffe, a 35-year-old lorry driver, was led from a van with a blanket over his head before being remanded in custody. His wife, Sonia, was reported to have left the courtroom in tears, with her father-in-law, Jack Sutcliffe. The 30-year-old art teacher had remained composed in court for the nine-minute hearing. Sutcliffe stood in the dock with his head bowed as he was charged.

The white pebble-dashed house where Peter Sutcliffe lived was besieged by sightseers as his identity became known. Garden Lane, Heaton, Bradford, was swarming with people wanting to see the house where Sutcliffe and his wife had lived in seclusion. He was a loner at the engineering firm where he worked, and a neighbour said he hardly ever saw them together. He was often away from home, when his work as a lorry driver took him to other parts of the country, and he spent his spare time working on his car. The couple had married in August 1974 and had no children. It was thought that the Sutcliffes were planning to move from the area to a small country property, but that their house didn't sell and they remained in Heaton.

In January 2011, a *Mirror* reporter recalled how he had "... unmasked Peter Sutcliffe ..." 30 years before. He said: "An address which would soon be notorious across the world – 6 Garden Lane – was the last house I went to.

"When I saw a police car parked outside, the only vehicle or sign of life in the street, I made a big Biro tick in my notebook. But even without the police car, 6 Garden Lane seemed oddly spooky. In a road of ordinary 1930s semis, it was tall and detached and set high above the street. In the yellow streetlight, it looked grey and forbidding. So this was the home of the Yorkshire Ripper. We had imagined the ogre would live in a seedy bedsit, not a middle-class detached house in one of the best parts of Bradford. Heart in mouth, I knocked at number 6, but the house was clearly empty. So I tried number 4, the only neighbour. An elderly chap answered.

"I explained that I was a reporter and his neighbour was probably going to be charged with the Ripper murders in the morning. The man, Tom Garside, couldn't have been more welcoming. It turned out Tom and his wife Mary had been convinced for months that their strange neighbour was the Ripper, but couldn't get the police interested. My mouth fell open as the Garsides talked about Sutcliffe. Here, my shorthand deteriorates as it goes along, such was my excitement at the details emerging.

"He was a lorry driver, they said, and his wife Sonia was a supply teacher. The Sutcliffes were 'a queer sort of couple' but good enough neighbours. Mary told me: 'He has an old Rover he works on a lot. He goes out late after other people have gone to bed, and he doesn't come back until the morning.' 'The strangest thing,' said Tom, 'was that he often used to burn his clothes on a bonfire in the garden and it always seemed to be after one of the murders.'

"A Rover was the car identified as being driven suspiciously after the Jacqueline Hill murder. As for burning his clothes, this was astonishing stuff.

"Tom Garside had evidence of disagreements within the West Yorkshire police over Sutcliffe. The story that was already unfolding was to have political repercussions for years afterwards. There were policemen, it was revealed in official reports after he was convicted, who were convinced Sutcliffe was the Ripper. That night, Tom told me: 'Last spring, I heard a heated discussion on the front drive. An officer was saying to Sutcliffe, "I've had enough of this, you're coming with us." But when we contacted the police to tell them we think it's him, they say if he's not a Geordie, we're not interested.' [The police were convinced by the famous hoax Ripper tape that the wanted man was a Geordie, so Sutcliffe, with his Bradford accent, was repeatedly ruled out.]

"'You know, there's somebody you should try to find,' Mary

Garside said conspiratorially as she came in with cups of tea. She had in her hand a scrap of paper with the name 'Szurma' and a phone number. 'Sonia's mother', she said.

"The Garsides declined for the rest of their lives to speak to reporters, apart from one background interview they gave to a young, local BBC researcher, Mark Byford, who later became the BBC's deputy director-general. With my notebook full of the Garsides' revelations, I was desperate to phone in the information I had, as it was close to the last possible moment to get news into the next morning's paper. I now wondered how I would find the elusive Mrs Szurma, whose phone number I had. It was several hours before we got a breakthrough.

"A colleague, with the help of a friend at the telephone exchange, got an address to match the number. All over Yorkshire, relieved and delighted people, it seemed, were prepared to break rules that night to help uncover the trail of Peter Sutcliffe. It was 2 a.m. when I reached Tanton Crescent, where Mrs Szurma lived. I was now with one of my favourite colleagues, photographer David Parry. Again, we were out on our own. We knocked on the door and a grey-haired man – Sutcliffe's father-in-law, Bodhan Szurma – leaned out of an upstairs window. 'Yes, what is it?' he asked in an East European accent. In a loud whisper, I explained I was a reporter and wanted to talk about Peter.

"'Is it the car thing?' he replied. We later learned from the police that Sutcliffe was due in court over some motoring offences which would affect his livelihood. But it was strange that Mr Szurma was so calm about being woken at 2am by journalists to discuss such a minor thing. 'No,' I replied. 'It's a bit more serious. He's in a bit of trouble.' Mr Szurma said he would come down.

"I heard years later that Sonia Sutcliffe had excused Peter for his crimes, but would never forgive the local reporter who broke the news to her parents.

"We spent an hour or so in the Szurmas' little kitchen. It was a poor but proud and respectable household. They made us tea, with used teabags which had been dried out on top of the cooker. Bodhan, a Czech, stood impassive in his brown dressing gown. His wife Maria was more emotional. 'Petey, our Petey,' she shrieked. Then she said it was impossible Peter could have been under arrest for two days as Sonia had phoned that day and said they would be round for tea on Monday.

"It seems she was still shielding them from the shock for as long as possible. Bodhan said the police had the wrong man. He reached into a drawer for a red plastic photo album, which he opened at pictures of his son-in-law by a Christmas tree with some kids. 'Can you tell me that is the face of a murderer?' he demanded. 'It's crazy, ridiculous.' Both of us, plus another colleague who had arrived and squeezed into the kitchen, were looking at the photos and thinking the same thing – that the bearded man in the recently taken photos was the image of several of the Photofit pictures that had been issued over the years of the Ripper. We could hardly say this to his parents-in-law, though. Bodhan pressed the album into my hands.

"'Take this to the police station,' he said. 'Put it in your newspaper.

People will realise they have the wrong man.' We left, aware that we had the most sought-after photos in the world in our hands, although the best of them were never published. Sonia fought a lengthy copyright battle over them and they were eventually returned to her. Over the coming weeks, I was privy to journalistic coup after coup, all through [my boss's] patronage rather than my skill.

"One day we were invited to a police garage where investigators had collected from across the country all the shabby old cars Sutcliffe had used in his murders. After almost every killing, there had been reports of a car thought to have been used by the murderer. And here they were ... the brown Rover from the last killing ... the white Ford Corsair from another ... the black Capri and so on. I went back to Bradford last week to walk around Garden Lane and Tanton Crescent. Astonishingly, Sonia still lives at number 6, where she's known as a recluse who stays behind thick, drawn curtains and never answers the door. As I turned to go, I glimpsed her through her kitchen window. Our eyes even met for a second or two. I doubt she had any idea I was that hated local journalist from 30 years ago."

On 20th February 1981, Peter Sutcliffe stood in a packed courtroom accused of murdering 13 women and attempting to murder seven others. Sutcliffe admitted killing 13 women, but it was up to the jury to decide if he was mentally unbalanced, or a clever liar. The killer had pleaded not guilty to 13 charges of murder, but guilty of manslaughter on the grounds of diminished responsibility. He also pleaded guilty to seven charges of attempted murder. All the doctors who examined the Yorkshire Ripper agreed that he was suffering from paranoid schizophrenia, but there was a marked difference between the story he told the doctors and the one he told police. He told doctors that God made him do it. He said the voices "from God" convinced him that he was on a divine mission. He believed he was ridding the world of "scum" and he also convinced himself that the women he attacked and killed were all sex workers. But the killings had a clear badge of identity. All the victims suffered skull fractures and were repeatedly stabbed, often in the same wound, and as the number of murders and attacks rose, Sutcliffe slipped through the police net nine times. Each time he was interviewed about his car being seen in red-light areas, he came up with an explanation. He claimed after his arrest that being tricked out of £10 by a sex worker was what fuelled his hatred for them. In almost every case, Sutcliffe had removed the victim's clothes before stabbing her, and told police that he did this so that when they were found they would "look as cheap as they are". In court, Sir Michael Havers, prosecuting, stood behind a table on which weapons including hammers, knives and screwdrivers were placed. He warned the jury that they would have to look at photographs of the victims and "steel yourselves". Sutcliffe admitted to stabbing the women in their hearts, lungs and throats because "you can kill them quicker that way". Emily Jackson was stabbed 52 times. He told police he killed Patricia Atkinson because he heard her using foul language. He said: "It was obvious why I picked her up. No decent woman would have been using language like that at the top of her voice." The jury was told how Sutcliffe had used a hacksaw to try to sever Jean Jordan's head. Sutcliffe had sexual intercourse with only one of his victims, Helen Rytka, an 18-year-old sex worker from Bradford. Apparently, he had intercourse in an attempt to calm her down after a first attempt to kill her had failed. When the jury saw photos of Vera Millward, one of them had to be removed before the folder of pictures was given to them because it was so distressing. Josephine Whitaker was killed with a sharpened screwdriver, which was thrust deep inside her vagina three times.

An evil hoax had seriously hampered the investigation, Sir Michael Havers told the Old Bailey. Sutcliffe had been ruled out of the inquiry on a number of occasions because his handwriting and voice did not match the letters and tapes sent to police by hoaxers. A psychiatric report explained that Sutcliffe's control and his wife's cold personality contributed to a detachment from the offences.

It had taken police 15 hours and 40 minutes to take down the statement from Sutcliffe. The turning point had come as he'd stabbed Wilma McCann after hitting her over the head with a hammer. He said: "After that first time I developed and played up a hatred for prostitutes in order to justify within myself a reason why I had attacked and killed Wilma McCann." He then recalled how his wife was in bed when he got home. He noticed blood on his jeans which he rinsed in the kitchen and hung up. He wiped blood off his boots before going to bed. "I then carried on as if nothing had happened," the statement continued. The case for the prosecution came to an end on 9th May 1981. During the defence, Sutcliffe told the courtroom that he had known that the police had suspected him on a number of occasions, but there just wasn't enough proof to tie him to the crimes. In court, he also said that he would kill more women if he was ever set free. Asked why, he explained that his divine mission to rid the streets of prostitutes was not yet completed. He also claimed that he wasn't mad, but a top psychiatrist later told the Old Bailey jury that he believed the serial killer was suffering from paranoid schizophrenia. The psychiatrist was then asked if Sutcliffe could be feigning it, having copied his wife's behaviour when she was known to have suffered from the illness before their marriage. Dr Hugo Milne told the court he thought it highly unlikely that Sutcliffe could simulate mental illness. Prison officers responsible for Sutcliffe while he was on remand were convinced that all the medical experts were being duped by the killer.

As the trial continued, sex worker Marcella Claxton, who survived a brutal assault by the Ripper, was refused compensation because of her profession. Marcella needed 52 stitches and lost the baby she was carrying when Sutcliffe attacked her with a hammer in Leeds. Despite Sutcliffe admitting he tried to kill the young woman, and Marcella still suffering from pain caused by the injuries five year earlier, she wasn't entitled to any money for the ordeal she'd been through. Following all the medical expert witnesses, Sir Michael Havers, QC, said that if Sutcliffe was "feigning mental illness he was 'a sadistic, calculated cold-blooded murderer who loved his job'." Meanwhile, the part that Sonia Sutcliffe had had to play came to light. She was described as a cold woman who had provoked her husband on occasion. She had been obsessed with cleanliness and insisted her husband wash his own clothes, but he couldn't use the washing machine. She also made him take his boots off before entering the house. Whether her "nagging" had contributed to the tragic chain of events was up for debate. Sutcliffe had never mentioned his "divine mission" to the police, only to the doctors who were examining him and it was strongly suggested that he was simply making it up.

The judge, Mr Justice Borham, gave his summing up on 21st May 1981, but decided to send the jury out the following day. The judge said that the defence contained three essential ingredients and the jury had to answer three vital questions. The first was whether Sutcliffe was suffering from a mental abnormality at the time of each of the 13 killings, the second concerned the claim that he was being directed by God, while the third question was whether the man's abnormality was enough to substantially impair his mental responsibility for his acts. If the jury decided that he wasn't suffering from an abnormality, then they had to find him guilty of murder.

Peter Sutcliffe was jailed on 22nd May 1981, on what would have been Jacqueline Hill's 21st birthday. He was found guilty of the murder of 13 women and sentenced to life imprisonment of at least 30 years as recommended by the judge. At 4.22 p.m., the foreman of the Old Bailey jury returned the first verdict: guilty of murder. It took a total of five minutes to bring in 12 more verdicts of guilty of murder. In the end, despite the lengthy evidence of three psychiatrists, the jury of six men and six women decided by a majority of 10 to two that he was a murderer and not a madman. An evil coward, not a man with a mission.

Sonia Sutcliffe however, who was questioned by police for 12 hours following her husband's arrest, assured them that she knew nothing of his crimes. Sutcliffe had lied and cheated when it came to Sonia and told her countless lies. He claimed he hated pornography, but that too was a lie. He was a regular reader of pornographic magazines and he hid his obsession with the vice world and his bloodlust for sex workers. These weren't the only lies he told. He wooed divorcee Theresa Douglas with love letters and told her that his wife had died in a car accident. He asked the woman to marry him. For two years he maintained a relationship with Theresa before Sonia began to suspect there was another woman and he promised to end it. He joined the labourers in greasy overalls at strip shows in Belle Vue and at the Gaiety Bar in Chapeltown, Leeds, where he was fascinated by vice. He had joined the kerb-crawlers by the time he was 18.

After he went to prison, Sutcliffe was questioned over the unsolved murder of 24-year-old teacher Barbara Mayo, who was strangled after she thumbed a lift from London to the north in 1970. She was picked up by the driver of a Morris 1000 (Sutcliffe drove that model at the time) and the convicted serial killer was known to have visited Sonia while she studied in London. Detectives thought he would have realized he had nothing to lose by telling the truth. In June 1981, however, the killer sought an appeal against his 13 convictions for murder. He was sticking to his earlier claim that he had committed manslaughter with diminished responsibility. He lost his appeal in May 1982.

Early in 1983, Sutcliffe was slashed four times with a piece of jagged glass by another inmate at Parkhurst prison on the Isle of Wight, scarring him for life. There were moves to get the killer moved to a secure psychiatric unit. He was moved to Broadmoor in 1984 under the Mental Health Act, where he saw himself as a "victim". Nine years later he said: "The terrible hate-inspiring nickname The Yorkshire Ripper is a misnomer by the media calculated to evoke as much ignorance and hatred as they could possibly extract from people. The fact is I am not a terrible person but I have had some terrible ex-experiences and I trust the reader [of the autobiography he intended to write – *The Way it Was*], will bear with me and read without bias whilst I open my mind. Every time I see an article in tabloid-type newspapers I can feel the ignorance, malice and hatred. It's deliberate and horrible and because they have no idea as to what I'm really like, it often makes me wish I was dead to make everybody happy! Then on the other hand it stirs up inside me the determination to try to keep going. I am compelled to write this twin volume autobiography type of book. I believe that people should want to know what exactly has gone on in the mind of someone who has always been polite and caring and yet at the same time could have done things totally out of character and against his own nature! How many people reading this think they know about my thoughts and my situation? A great many I'll wager! But you do not! – apart from the fact that I admitted being responsible for 13 killings and seven attempts and was sentenced to life imprisonment, basically that is all you know!"

Sutcliffe was aggrieved about some of the things that had been written and wanted to present himself as better than that. The only visitor to see Sutcliffe alone in the mid-1990s was Chief Constable Keith Hellawell, who said: "I go there to talk about specific purposes. Whether people are born evil or become evil is without prediction. Each one of us is capable of murder. But we would not kill like a serial killer kills unless something happened to us. 'Mad' is seen by people as staring eyes, irrational behaviour, traits that are not apparent in serial killers I have spoken to." In 1995, Sutcliffe admitted that he conned experts into thinking he was mad in order to keep his life of luxury in Britain's top-security hospital. He told his former nurse, whose job it was to counsel and nurse him, that there were no voices in his head and no voice of God. The debate as to whether Peter Sutcliffe should be in prison or remain in a top-security hospital raged on for the next 15 years.

Another piece of the case was closed in February 2006 when a jobless divorcee admitted that he had been the Ripper tape hoaxer, Wearside Jack. John Humble, 50, confessed to sending the taunting tape and three letters, including one to the *Mirror*. It was this diabolical hoax that meant police failed to take more notice of other vital clues, and left the Ripper free to kill at least three more women. Humble was arrested in Sunderland, and was jailed for eight years in March 2006. In a sensational move, Sutcliffe wrote to Humble and blamed him for the three deaths that could have been avoided had police not been thrown off the trail by the hoaxer.

It had started with a murder that went mostly unremarked –

but it was the start of a nightmare that would last years and terrify millions of women across the nation. When Sutcliffe lost his attempt to challenge an order that he can never be released in March 2011, it brought some relief to the families of his victims and to those victims who had survived horrific ordeals at the hands of one of Britain's most notorious murderers, the Yorkshire Ripper.

However, the killer was back in the press in October 2013, when it was reported that he could be responsible for a further murder, his fourteenth. Alison Morris, 25, was stabbed to death in 1979 at the height of Peter Sutcliffe's killing spree. Detectives at the time ruled out the possibility that Alison was a victim of the Ripper, but the case is unsolved. Retired cop Chris Clark now says he has unearthed new evidence linking Sutcliffe to the murder and believes he may have killed even more women. Chris, an officer for more than 30 years, said: "I feel Alison's murder was committed by Peter Sutcliffe because of the frenzied nature of the attack.

"I feel very strongly he was disturbed in the act of going further. There may have been other people in the woods who he saw or heard, so he got away before he finished."

Alison was stabbed repeatedly in the chest with a knife on 1st September 1979, as she went for a walk near her home in Ramsey, Essex.

Just seven hours later, Sutcliffe murdered 20-year-old student Barbara Leach in Bradford, West Yorkshire. Detectives believed Barbara's death proved the Ripper did not kill Alison. But Chris found the trucker's work often took him to the port of Harwich, just miles from Alison's home. The former intelligence officer reckons Sutcliffe may have murdered the two women on the same day.

He said: "Alison went out on September 1st for a walk by the River Stour and was later found murdered – stabbed repeatedly in the chest with a single-bladed knife.

"Seven hours later, Barbara Leach was murdered by Sutcliffe in Bradford after he parked his lorry and got in his car. It was 216 miles from Ramsey to his depot, so it is quite feasible that seven hours earlier he murdered Alison." Chris Clark's research has also unearthed evidence from a couple who owned a garden furniture shop near Alison's home. They believe they saw Sutcliffe in the area at around the time of the murder – but cannot be sure it was the exact date. Chris added: "They described a driver of a lorry who pulled up and asked directions for Harwich one day. They described Peter Sutcliffe and after his arrest they saw his photo on the TV and said he was the man."

A post-mortem found Alison was the victim of an "extremely vicious attack". Chris, who served with Norfolk Police, added: "Alison's is one of 17 cases I am looking at which are still unsolved and no one seems to care about." Essex police's cold case team said all unsolved crimes were reviewed and they looked at any new information. Chris planned to present his dossier of evidence to the Home Office. Alison's mum, Mavis Morris, was too upset to comment on Chris Clark's claims. She said: "I still find it too upsetting to speak about."

Michael Brookes

1978

A schoolboy claimed that he helped stab a girl to protect his mum. It was 7th November 1978 and Roy Brookes told a stunned court room he was frightened his stepfather would harm his mother if he refused. Brookes was accused of the "ripper-style" killing of 16-year-old Lynn Siddons in a wood near Derby. Lynn was stabbed repeatedly after being lured there by the 15-year-old youngster. But Brookes, from Derby, denied murder. He claimed that he tricked Lynn into the wood on the orders of his stepfather Michael Brookes. Then, he alleges, he was forced to take part in an attack carefully planned by Mr Brookes. However, his stepfather denied connection with the killing and was not charged. The boy's mother wept as she sat at the back of Nottingham Crown Court while her son gave evidence. Brookes said that his stepfather had talked of Jack the Ripper and they had seen a film about him. He saw his stepfather stabbing pictures of women in books. When his stepfather saw a woman out walking, he would threaten "to get her". Brookes' QC, Douglas Draycott asked: "What did you understand him to mean?" The boy replied: "He wanted to kill her." He was then asked: "How did you feel?" "Scared, I didn't want to do anything," came the reply. The boy added: "Dad said if we didn't get one we would have to get my mother." Referring to the attack, Brookes said he hit Lynn with a carving knife that broke. Then his stepfather told him to use another knife. He added: "I just did it lightly. Lynn fell to the floor. I never touched her again. Dad took the knife from me. He was sticking it in her. Then he held her under some water. I was trying not to look."

The man accused by Roy Brookes of a vicious murder declared: "I'm not a killer." Michael Brookes hit out after Roy was cleared of the ripper killing of Lynn, who was stabbed repeatedly. He stood accused by the boy of planning a vicious attack and delivering the killer blows. Thirty-three-year-old Brookes said: "My conscience is clear. Tongues may wag and fingers point, but I don't give two hoots. The way things have turned out for Roy I don't blame him for making up the story. There may have been another person there, but it certainly wasn't me." By this time, Brookes had been questioned by police for 48 hours. He was released without being charged. Doris Brookes, 31, said: "I believe in Roy – and I can't say that my husband was responsible. I stood by my son. Now, despite all the gossip, I shall stand by my husband." However, Lynn's grandmother, Florence Siddons, who lived in the same street in Derby as the Brookes family, said: "Our girl is dead. The maniac – and I'm sure I know who did it – is walking free." It was thought that Mrs Siddons would take out a private prosecution as she vowed: "We'll not let the matter rest." Lynn's battered body was found in the wood after she vanished on a walk with Roy. He then confessed in a statement to stabbing her, but later claimed his stepfather was the one who actually butchered the girl after talking about wanting to kill more women than Jack the Ripper. Roy was taken into care by social services, while a police spokesman said the file was still open.

One week after the court case, Michael Brookes refused to let Roy take a truth drug and explained: "If they are going to work like that, this country is getting like Russia. I don't believe in that sort of thing. I just have no faith in the medical profession." Brookes and his wife were known to have moved from their house on Carlisle Street in Derby following Roy's trial. However, widowed Florence Siddons refused to let the matter go and at the age of 66 turned detective in the hunt for her granddaughter's killer. Meanwhile, the Director of Public Prosecutions studied Mrs Siddons' dossier, but said there was no new evidence to justify a charge.

Four years later, in March 1982, the Lynn Siddons murder case was reopened. Lynn had been found in scrubland with 30 gashes in the stomach and throat, and at this point a new set of papers with regard to her murder was on its way to the Director of Public Prosecutions. Top detectives from Derbyshire, led by Chief Superintendent John Reddington, Commander of Alfreton police station, and Superintendent Roy Morton, planned to travel to London for talks with the DPP. Soon after Lynn's body was found in undergrowth at Sinfin, police charged Roy, but his acquittal took the jury just 20 minutes to decide. For the previous four years nothing happened, but the victim's family campaigned tirelessly for more urgent police action to find and charge the real killer. When a new Chief Constable was appointed in 1981, Alfred Parrish promised to reopen the case for the family and told them that all the evidence would be thoroughly investigated once again. For the six months prior to the reopening of the case, Derbyshire detectives had interviewed a number of people about the case. They also unearthed a great deal of new evidence and took statements from people who did not appear at Roy Brookes' trial.

In early March 1982, a preliminary report was sent to the DPP, which was followed by further papers, and a full-scale meeting with police officers was set up. Florence Siddons, who had brought Lynn up, said: "I'm delighted by the news. I hope they will sort this out at last." In November the following year, it was reported that a new witness had come forward with startling new facts about the macabre murder. By now it was established that Roy Brookes had claimed that while out walking with Lynn, Michael Brookes had grabbed the young girl – one of his neighbours – from behind and had stabbed and strangled her to death. Brookes had been unable to account for his whereabouts at the time the youngsters were walking. And, two years after Lynn's death, Doris Brookes made a statement to lawyers acting for the murdered girl's family saying that her husband was obsessed by a combination of knives and sex and that he had been out on the afternoon of the murder. She also told the lawyers that Michael Brookes had changed his trousers as soon as he returned home that day. The trousers had blood on them, said the statement, and were promptly burned. A year later, Mrs Brookes stated that her husband had confessed to the murder. The same statement was made to Derby police, but "Mick" Brookes was not charged. The couple had split up for a time, but when Brookes came back to live with his wife in late 1980, she withdrew her statement, saying she had made it up because she was jealous of another woman. The couple moved to a council house in Peterborough and were living under an assumed name.

However, new evidence uncovered by the former Labour MP for Derby North, Philip Whitehead, showed that Doris Brookes had made a strikingly similar statement a week after the murder. Whitehead, who had pursued the case for five years, interviewed a man who said he had visited Doris Brookes on the day her husband and son were first taken to a police station. The man was accompanied by his mother, his stepfather and his then girlfriend. Whitehead passed their names to Derby police. Only one of the four people, a divorced woman in her late thirties, agreed to make a statement. She was interviewed by Detective Inspector Jim Payne and claimed: "I made my statement because I feel very, very sorry for the Siddons family." She continued: "At the time of Lynn's murder I was friendly with a man who was close to Mick Brookes and his wife. When we heard that Roy had been arrested I drove this man and his parents to the police station. They would not let us see Roy or Mick. So we drove straight from there to Dot's house. We were there for about an hour.

"She was in a terrible state shouting out all the time how sorry she was for Roy, and how wrong it was of Mick to involve Roy. She said nobody knew what a life she'd had. She said she had often been forced to have sex with a knife at her throat. She said there were marks all over the wallpaper which had been torn when Mick had thrown knives at pin-ups stuck on the walls." The woman said that she had queried Doris Brookes about the fact that there would have been a lot of blood. She was told that there was a great deal of blood on her husband's trousers, but that they burnt them. Speaking four years after the crime, the woman said she was extremely surprised that the police had not spoken to her earlier as they knew her connection with the Brookes family. While a spokesman for the DPP confirmed that some new evidence had come to light, it hadn't changed the decision to take no action. In an angry outburst, Florence Siddons said: "It stinks. It has been a cover-up from start to finish. And that's not just the family's opinion. It's what Derby people think too." Philip Whitehead said: "I wonder how many years have to go by and how many more witnesses we have to find before the amazingly obvious fact that all the evidence points to one direction breaks through to the police and the DPP."

A bitter dispute between Merseyside police and Derby police broke out towards the end of July 1985, some seven years after Lynn's murder, which then took a turn for the worse. Six weeks earlier, senior officers from Merseyside police were called in to investigate a complaint against Derby police by Lynn's grandmother. Merseyside police recommended a new inquiry into the murder – under a police force outside Derbyshire – but it was angrily resisted by the local police who refused to accept the recommendation. A new witness in the case who gave a crucial statement to Merseyside police was then interviewed again by the local force, but later withdrew her statement. Carol Dunsworth went to live with Mick Brookes a year after the murder, and left him about a year after that. Brookes still couldn't account for his movements on the afternoon of the murder, but Dunsworth told Merseyside police that he had confessed to her that he was the murderer of Lynn. He admitted meeting Roy and Lynn on their walk, and to stabbing the young girl. He also said that Roy had joined in and that they had left her body in the undergrowth while the victim was still alive. It was this statement that formed the basis of the recommendation that the inquiry should be reopened. However, soon after the decision was taken not to reopen the inquiry, Carol Dunsworth told Derby police that the statement to the Liverpool force had been made "under duress" and that she had made up lies to get rid of them. Apparently, though, her statement had been given freely and she made no complaint about the way it was taken until the Derbyshire police intervened. She confirmed all the facts to the press, but refused to comment on them.

By 1987, Florence had been fighting for nine years to see justice for her murdered granddaughter. In April that year, she won her fight to take Mick Brookes to court for battery. She claimed that the man, by now living under an assumed name in Peterborough, was guilty of the "brutal and sexually perverted murder". It had taken a marathon battle to get this far, but backed by the *Mirror*, Mrs Siddons now had legal aid to get the man she believed responsible into court. If the Siddons family won their civil action, it would certainly force the police to reopen the case. Florence said: "At last we can take action against Brookes. We are absolutely delighted. This gives us the chance to bring this all out in the open in a court case. And, that is what the police should have done years ago". She added: "The last nine years have been a nightmare. Now we have a chance to find out who killed Lynn." In the writ, the family claimed: "She suffered agonising pain and terror before she died." Having been a prosecution witness against Roy Brookes at his trial, Brookes now faced his own time in the dock, accused of inflicting up to 40 knife wounds on an innocent teenager. However, Brookes insisted he was innocent. In a statement issued by his solicitor, he said that he "wholly and completely" rejected the allegations. Brookes, who was now known as Goodwood, intended to defend the action.

On 5th May 1988, Brookes' lawyers applied to strike out an action by Gail Halford, Lynn Siddons' mother. Halford too, was to sue the man for battery, but his lawyers claimed the writ was too late, and was "scandalous, frivolous, vexatious and an abuse of the process of the court." But the case continued when the action to strike was refused. It continued, in fact, for a number of years. In 1990, journalist of the year Paul Foot, from the *Mirror*, claimed a victory after his 10-year backing of Gail Halford to bring her daughter's killers to justice. The High Court told Gail that she could sue the two men she believed responsible. Legal history would be made when Brookes and his stepson faced civil action for damages (due in 1991). It would be the first time that a family of a murder victim had sued without the defendants being found guilty in a criminal court. The men faced claims for aggravated damages, damages for the fatal battery of Lynn, and damages for her "lost years". If Mrs Halford won her case, then the police would be forced, once again, to consider reopening the case. Lynn's family vowed they would fight on. Florence said: "We have got to see justice done." She had arrived in the office of Paul Foot 10 years earlier and begged him to campaign for justice. Florence felt that even at the time of the murder the police had done everything they could to obstruct each move to prosecute Mick Brookes. At first, Foot didn't believe her, but then he read the facts.

Roy Brookes was an illiterate five and a half stone lad, who the judge at the original trial did not believe had the strength to asphyxiate Lynn. He said at the time: "Does not the evidence all point to there being someone else there at the time as well as this young man, and that someone was strong enough to asphyxiate Lynn?" Foot also looked at the fact that Brookes could not account for his movements on the afternoon in question. He was also known to throw knives at pictures of naked women, he was obsessed with Jack the Ripper and he forced Doris Brookes to be prodded with knives during sexual foreplay and intercourse. She had told police that Brookes had said: "I did kill Lynn and I fucking enjoyed it." The Siddons family felt that the police refused to charge Mick Brookes because they didn't want to be shown up as bunglers. Foot's first article about the case came in January 1981. But it was vetoed by lawyers because they said they had never known of a published article suggesting a named man had committed a murder which he denied. It took him three months to convince them otherwise when he presented them with evidence and more facts. After that, Foot wrote nine articles which outlined the four witnesses who implicated Brookes, the recommendation of Merseyside police that the case should be reopened, the refusal in 1985 of the Director of Public Prosecutions to prosecute, and the fact that Mr Justice

Schiemann, in the High Court, refused to allow the case to go ahead when the family won the writ. At the time, he reported that a sobbing Mrs Siddons had said: "Do they really want a child-killer to go free rather than admit a mistake?" But the Court of Appeal unanimously overturned the Schiemann judgment who felt it should be ascertained if the Brookeses were lying.

The High Court judgment in the 13-year battle for justice was due on Monday 30th September 1991. In the interim years, the family had filed for criminal compensation for the loss of Lynn's life. They were awarded a paltry £27.00 by the Criminal Injuries Board – which two *Mirror* journalists wrote was insulting, and "only added to their pain". The 13 years of campaigning had kept every sickening detail of what happened to Lynn fresh in the minds of her family. The fact that Lynn had been repeatedly stabbed, with soil in her mouth that had been rammed there by her killer, while she was held with her face in a muddy puddle and strangled when she refused to die quickly, had given her mother nightmares for many years. When Lynn was found by schoolboys, and the body reported to police, it quickly became clear that her clothes were awry due to the killer's frantic efforts to grope her while she was being killed.

Gail Halford won her battle to "nail the brute" who murdered her daughter that same afternoon. A judge branded "knife fiend" Michael Brookes as the killer of Lynn Siddons. It was a historic civil case in which Gail was awarded damages. She blasted "bungling police" for failing to bring the killer to justice, and Derbyshire police admitted that they had made a mess of the case. An urgent meeting was planned with the Director of Public Prosecutions who would decide whether to bring a charge. Following the victory, Mrs Halford said: "We would like to thank Paul Foot and the *Daily Mirror* for believing us, supporting us and printing our story when the police and so many other people were against us." The judge had said: "I am left in no reasonable doubt that Michael Brookes killed Lynn Siddons."

As Gail Halford and Florence Siddons celebrated their victory at the High Court in London, a desperate Michael Brookes bitterly protested his innocence from the bathroom window of his home. He shouted: "I am innocent, always have been and have been saying that for 13 years." He vowed: "I will clear my name when the time comes." He claimed in a TV interview that the last 13 years of his life had been hell.

On 1st October 1991, the "knife fiend" finally nailed for the murder of Lynn sat silent and stony-faced in court while his lawyer did the talking. Solicitor Anthony Wharton said Michael Brookes was under "enormous strain". But he admitted that for him [now] to deny murdering Lynn would be "like spitting in the wind". The day before, he'd come out of hiding to complain of being hounded and he'd flung a torrent of abuse at reporters outside his terraced council house. His wife Doris "Dot" Brookes threatened a female radio reporter. He refused to answer questions, but his lawyer said he may appeal against the historic civil action ruling. His neighbours were also under pressure. One said: "If he's a killer we don't want him living here." In December 1991, Brookes was ordered to pay £10,000 damages to his victim's family.

Both Brookes and Roy Brookes denied murdering Lynn in 1996. However, the family didn't give up and in August 1996, Florence Siddons was in court to watch as Michael "Mick" Brookes, was jailed for life. Branded a "woman-hating pervert", he finally faced the reality of what he'd done, thanks to a crusade instigated by the murdered girl's family. Brookes had persuaded his then 15-year-old stepson to confess to the murder. Florence Siddons had stalked Brookes for many years. If she saw him in the street she'd shout: "You murdering bastard." She threw bricks through his windows, and sent him letters telling him what she wanted to do to him. As she stalked her quarry, Brookes and Doris moved home 14 times. He didn't dare leave his house, so he holed-up inside watching TV. Within days of moving, Florence would be standing outside. Her dedication to making Brookes' life a misery was unparalleled. It came to light that Brookes had bragged that he wanted to kill more victims than Jack the Ripper. He obsessively despised women, getting bizarre pleasure at the thought of dominating them. His fascination with the gory Ripper killings surfaced as a teenager. He would spend hours throwing knives at pin-ups covering the walls of his bedroom. He continued the sick habit until he killed Lynn. He also collected soft porn pictures, getting "evil pleasure" from mutilating them with a knife. One of three brothers, he'd had a disturbed childhood. He twice attempted suicide and was treated at a psychiatric hospital for depression. His marriage to Dominican-born Doris was turbulent and for a while he lived rough, and when he was at home, money was tight.

It was also revealed that police had bungled the investigation into Lynn's murder from day one. They allowed Brookes to spend time in a cell with his stepson and convince him to confess to the murder. They only made a scant examination of the murder scene and never searched the Brookes' garden. Later, a knife and clothing were found there, but they disappeared. A police report on the investigation is still secret.

The Ripper of Florence

1981

Police in Italy were hunting a ripper-style maniac who had killed up to six times in October 1981. He had preyed on couples making love in parked cars at secluded spots in the Tuscan hills around Florence. In the previous three months, two men and two women had been shot with a single .22 bullet in the back of the head, and the murders were an exact copy of the still-unsolved double killing committed in the same area in 1974. All the victims' bodies were mutilated with a scalpel, which appeared to have been used with the technique of a skilled surgeon. The latest couple to die at the killer's hands, according to police reports in 1981, were Susanna Cambi, 24, and her boyfriend, Stefano Baldi, 26. Florence investigating magistrate, Vincenzo Tricomi, said: "The monster is probably a peeping tom. If he is not a surgeon, he may be a butcher. He certainly has an expert knowledge of anatomy."

It seems that the crimes went back a long way, although they didn't begin with ripper killings. In August 1968, six-year-old Natalino Mele was asleep on the back seat of the car in which his mother, 32-year-old Barbara Locci, and her lover, 29-year-old Antonio Lo Bianco, were enjoying a sexual liaison when they were brutally shot dead by an unknown assailant. The child was either taken from the car by the killer and left on the doorstep of a nearby house at

10 THE PEOPLE, SUNDAY, OCTOBER 14, 1888.

THE SCENES OF THE RECENT MURDERS.

THE YARD OF THE "INTERNATIONAL AND EDUCATIONAL" CLUB, WHITECHAPEL. THE BODY WAS FOUND AT THE BACK OF THE OPEN DOOR.

When Last Seen Alive.

The Writing on the Wall.

MITRE-SQUARE, ALDGATE. THE SPOT WHERE THE BODY WAS FOUND IS MARKED BY A X

THE MITRE-SQUARE VICTIM. Inquest and Verdict.

What the Dead Woman's Daughter Says.

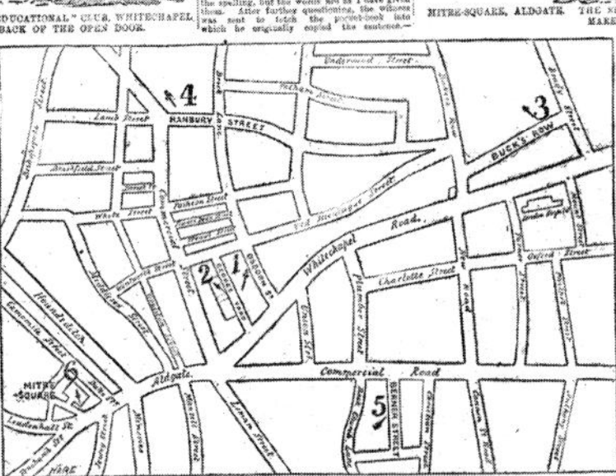

PLAN OF THE LOCALITY IN WHICH THE SIX WOMEN HAVE BEEN MURDERED SINCE APRIL LAST. THE PRECISE SPOT WHERE EACH CRIME WAS COMMITTED IS INDICATED BY A DAGGER AND A FIGURE.

Funeral of the Mitre-square Victim.

What the Bishop of Bedford Says.

Locked Up the Night Before.

The Search for Conway.

No Suspicious Sounds Heard.

Summing-up and Verdict.

Identity of the Berner-street Victim; The Real Mrs. Watts Found.

"Thieves' Candles": A Strange Superstition.

Jack the Ripper *The People* newspaper dated 14th October 1888 reports on the murders of Elizabeth Stride and Catherine Eddowes and includes a street plan showing the precise location where each of the Ripper's victims was found. They also published drawings of The International and Educational Club and Mitre Square, where the bodies of the latest two victims were found.

George Chapman (real name Severin Klosowski) was a suspect in the Jack the Ripper hunt.

Mary Ann "Polly" Nichols was one of Jack the Ripper's victims. Her body was discovered on 31st August 1888 in the Whitechapel area of London's East End.

Annie Chapman was another victim of Jack the Ripper.

Düsseldorf Ripper Peter Kürten, pictured with his wife, was suspected of crimes in numerous cities and earned the nickname the Düsseldorf Ripper.

"RIPPER'S" OWN STORY OF HIS CRIMES

GRIM RECITAL OF IMPULSE TO KILL

"I Was Embittered Against Humanity"

GIRL VICTIMS

Scissors Carried in His Pocket "To Stab Someone"

Some of the victims of the Dusseldorf murders, of which Peter Kuerten is accused. Left to right, Gertrude Hamacher, Luise Lenzen, Rudolf Scheer, Rosa Ohliger and Maria Hahn.

Accused of five murders and seven attempted murders, Peter Kuerten, aged forty-eight, when placed on trial at Dusseldorf yesterday, told the story of his life of crime.

With an amazing callousness, Kuerten related to the Court details of the terrible crimes he says he has committed.

The son of a drunken father, he said he was often in prison, and because of severe punishment became embittered against humanity.

Prominent criminologists and jurists from many countries are attending the trial.

5 MURDERS IN CHARGE

Kuerten's Amazing Disclosures in Terrible Story of His Life

DUSSELDORF, Monday.

During the reading of the indictment—sixteen crimes in all, including five murders and seven attempted murders—Kuerten remained "wooden." Then he told the terrible story of his life.

He was born forty-eight years ago of working-class parents in Mulheim. As a youth he was frequently in prison for theft.

Kuerten related the circumstances of the first murder on the list, that of Christina Klein, the nine-year-old daughter of a restaurant proprietor at Mulheim, on May 25, 1913, with a callousness which caused shudders in court.

He intended to steal something from one of the Kleins's bedrooms. In the second room he entered he saw little Christina lying peacefully in bed. He left a corpse.

Peter Kuerten.

He would not have killed the child, he said, but for the fact that vivid memories of his prison sufferings drove him to it.

The president asked Kuerten if he would describe the murders without going into too many revolting details. The accused agreed.

Kuerten then described assaults on men, women and children, speaking with a halting but calm voice. Describing his attempt to murder a married woman of fifty named Appelonia Kuehn, the second crime on the charge list, Kuerten admitted having a pair of scissors in his pocket with which to stab someone.

Five days later he left his dwelling at night in brutal mood. He saw Rosa Ohliger crying in a street of Slingern. He stabbed her to death.

On the second day he visited the body, intending to burn it by means of petrol, but he did not use the petrol until the following day. He wanted, as in the case of other victims, to gaze at the body.

He confirmed the details of Maria Hahn's murder and of her burial on the Papen[illegible]

Some of the Düsseldorf Ripper's victims. Peter Kürten was found guilty of nine murders and executed by guillotine in July 1931.

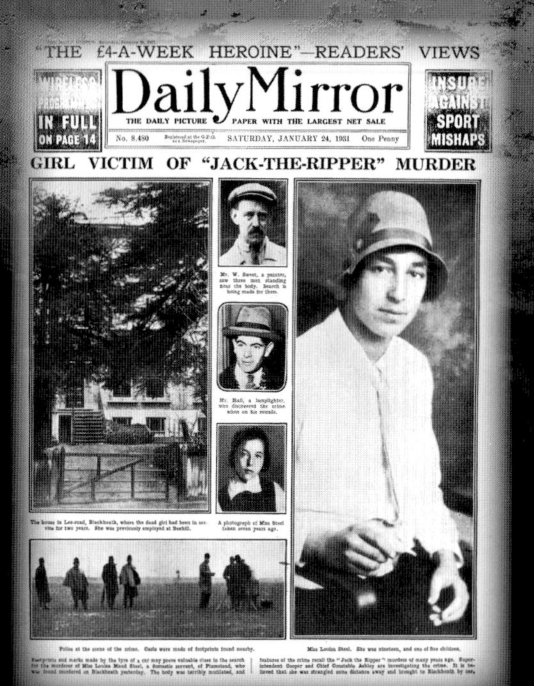
"THE £4-A-WEEK HEROINE"—READERS' VIEWS

WIRELESS PROGRAMMES IN FULL ON PAGE 14

Daily Mirror

THE DAILY PICTURE PAPER WITH THE LARGEST NET SALE

No. 8,480 Registered at the G.P.O. as a Newspaper. SATURDAY, JANUARY 24, 1931 One Penny

INSURE AGAINST SPORT MISHAPS

GIRL VICTIM OF "JACK-THE-RIPPER" MURDER

Mr. W. Sweet, a painter, saw three men standing near the body. Search is being made for them.

Mr. Hall, a lamplighter, who discovered the crime when on his rounds.

The house in Lee-road, Blackheath, where the dead girl had been in service for two years. She was previously employed at Bexhill.

A photograph of Miss Steel taken seven years ago.

Police at the scene of the crime. Casts were made of footprints found nearby.

Miss Louisa Steel. She was nineteen, and one of five children.

Footprints and marks made by the tyre of a car may prove valuable clues in the search for the murderer of Miss Louisa Maud Steel, a domestic servant, of Plumstead, who was found murdered on Blackheath yesterday. The body was terribly mutilated, and features of the crime recall the "Jack the Ripper" murders of many years ago. Superintendent Cooper and Chief Constable Ashley are investigating the crime. It is believed that she was strangled some distance away and brought to Blackheath by car,

Blackheath Ripp

The *Daily Mirror* reports on the dea of Louisa Steel in January 1931 at the hands of the Blackheath Ripper

The murder of Louisa Steel was one of 24 unsolved crimes ir three years.

XMAS TEAS FOR THE POOR—P. 18

Daily Mirror

Wireless on Page 14

THE DAILY PICTURE NEWSPAPER WITH THE LARGEST NET SALE

No. 8,759 Registered at the G.P.O. as a Newspaper. THURSDAY, DECEMBER 17, 1931 One Penny

TICH —PAGE 6

Christopher Stone To-morrow

DID YOU SEE VERA PAGE?

CHILD FOUND STRANGLED IN A GARDEN

The murdered girl and her mother and father.

Stowood Lodge, Addison-road, Kensington, in the front garden of which the body of Vera Page (left), aged ten, of Notting Hill, was found yesterday almost covered by earth. She had apparently been strangled. Right, Mr. Joseph Smith, a milk roundsman, who made the discovery. Scotland Yard have requested anyone who can give any information as to the child's whereabouts after 5 p.m. on Monday to communicate immediately with the police.

The murder of Vera Page made the front page of the national press in December 1931. Despite witness statements describing a suspicious man, the Blackheath Ripper was never brought to justice.

Blackout Ripper The Blackout Ripper was the nickname given to 28-year-old Gordon Frederick Cummins, an English serial killer who murdered four women in London in 1942.

Three of Cummins' victims – Evelyn Oatley (also known as Nita Ward), Doris Jouannet and Evelyn Margaret Hamilton. The Blackout Ripper was executed for his crimes in June 1942.

Note says victim No 3 will be a teenager

By ERNEST LEWIS

A "LAUGHING KILLER," who boasts that he has already stabbed two people to death has left a note on the doorstep of a police headquarters saying that he will claim a third victim—this time a teenager.

And detectives said last night: "We believe him. We are searching for a dangerous killer, a maniac."

Mrs. Marjorie Hill, 42 . . . stabbed to death

John Crossland, 44 . . . stabbed to death

Robert Whalley Marjorie Hill and John Crossland were victims of Robert Whalley.

Yorkshire Ripper A photofit of the Yorkshire Ripper issued by the police.

Assistant Chief Constable George Oldfield led the investigation into the Yorkshire Ripper murders.

Police search for clues in the murder of Jacqueline Hill who was attacked and brutally killed during a 200-yard walk to her flat from a bus stop in Leeds, 1980.

Police search a crime scene for bodies and evidence in the hunt for the Yorkshire Ripper, December 1980.

Peter Sutcliffe, the Yorkshire Ripper, leaves court in January 1981. The 35-year-old lorry driver from Bradford was suspected of carrying out 13 murders across West Yorkshire and Manchester.

Peter Sutcliffe sitting in the cab of his lorry at the Bradford engineering firm TW Clark, where he was employed as a driver. His job provided him with the opportunity to commit crimes in different areas.

Such was the depth of feeling over Sutcliffe's crimes that a lynch mob gathered outside the courthouse in Dewsbury, West Yorkshire.

A lucky escape! Olivia Reivers (left) was in the car with Sutcliffe when he was arrested while, minutes before, Denise Hall (right) had turned him away as she was instinctively suspicious about his behaviour.

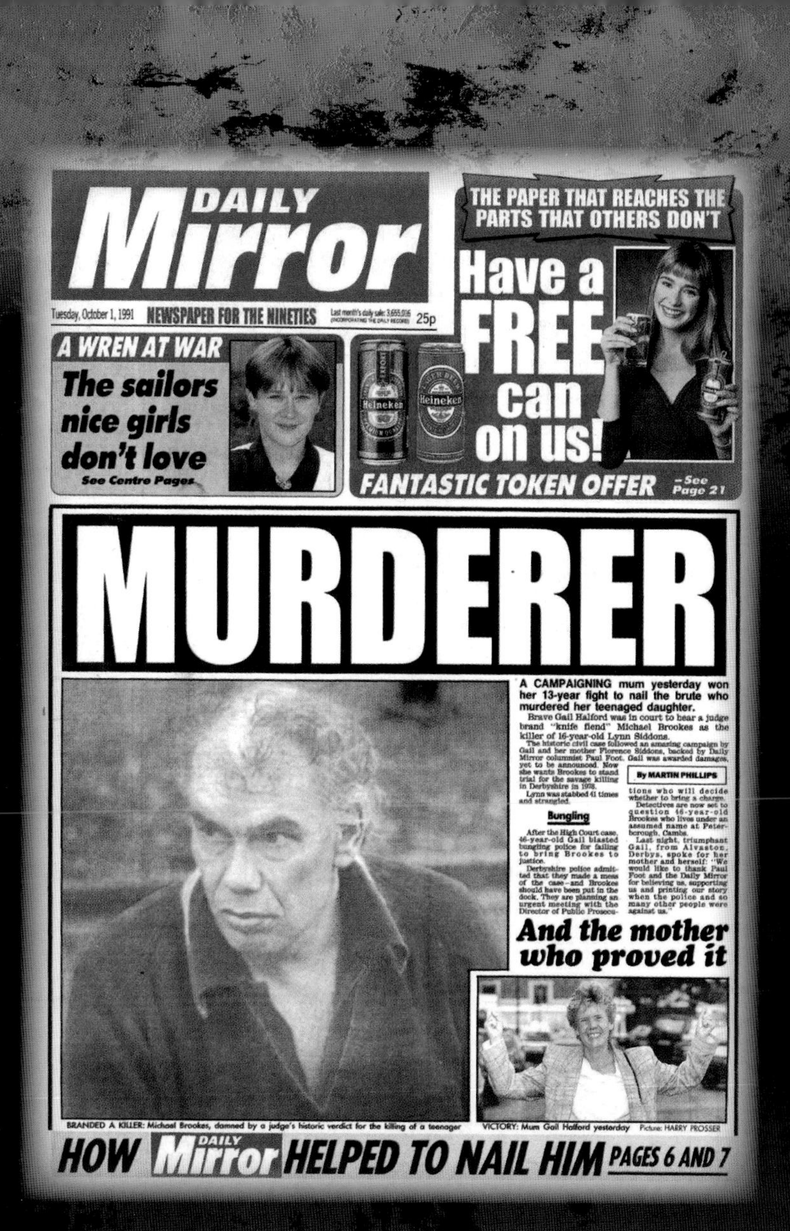

DAILY Mirror

Tuesday, October 1, 1991 NEWSPAPER FOR THE NINETIES Last month's daily sale: 3,655,016 (INCORPORATING THE DAILY RECORD) 25p

THE PAPER THAT REACHES THE PARTS THAT OTHERS DON'T

A WREN AT WAR

The sailors nice girls don't love

See Centre Pages

Have a FREE can on us!

FANTASTIC TOKEN OFFER – See Page 21

MURDERER

A CAMPAIGNING mum yesterday won her 13-year fight to nail the brute who murdered her teenaged daughter.

Brave Gail Halford was in court to hear a judge brand "knife fiend" Michael Brookes as the killer of 16-year-old Lynn Siddons.

The historic civil case followed an amazing campaign by Gail and her mother Florence Siddons, backed by Daily Mirror columnist Paul Foot. Gail was awarded damages, yet to be announced. Now she wants Brookes to stand trial for the savage killing in Derbyshire in 1978.

By MARTIN PHILLIPS

Lynn was stabbed 41 times and strangled.

Bungling

After the High Court case, 46-year-old Gail blasted bungling police for failing to bring Brookes to justice.

Derbyshire police admitted that they made a mess of the case – and Brookes should have been put in the dock. They are planning an urgent meeting with the Director of Public Prosecutions who will decide whether to bring a charge.

Detectives are now set to question 46-year-old Brookes who lives under an assumed name at Peterborough, Cambs.

Last night, triumphant Gail, from Alvaston, Derbys, spoke for her mother and herself: "We would like to thank Paul Foot and the Daily Mirror for believing us, supporting us and printing our story when the police and so many other people were against us."

And the mother who proved it

BRANDED A KILLER: Michael Brookes, damned by a judge's historic verdict for the killing of a teenager

VICTORY: Mum Gail Halford yesterday Picture: HARRY PROSSER

HOW DAILY Mirror HELPED TO NAIL HIM PAGES 6 AND 7

Michael Brookes Lynn Siddons' mother celebrates finally bringing Michael Brookes, the killer of her 16-year-old daughter, to justice.

Ransom Ripper Birmingham estate agent Stephanie Slater, who was kidnapped whilst showing a "prospective buyer" around a house, is pictured in January 1992 with her mother and father at a press conference after her employer paid the kidnapper the ransom to secure her release.

Stephanie Slater's ransom was collected near this bridge.

A police reconstruction shows the green bin on the left where Stephanie Slater was kept during her kidnap ordeal.

A police artist's picture of the man wanted in connection with the abduction of Stephanie Slater.

Michael Sams, dubbed the Ransom Ripper, was eventually convicted of the kidnapping of Stephanie Slater.

Michael Sams is taken to court to face charges of the attempted murder of probation officer Julia Flack.

Robert Napper The murder of Rachel Nickell on Wimbledon Common in July 1992 shocked the nation and triggered one of the biggest manhunts in recent police history.

Murder victim Rachel Nickell with her baby son Alex, Christmas 1989.

The area of Wimbledon Common where Rachel Nickell was viciously murdered.

Robert Napper arrives at the Old Bailey in December 2008 accused of murdering Rachel Nickell. He was already serving life for the murder of Samantha Bisset and her four-year-old daughter Jazmine.

Robert Napper, a schoolboy in the 1980s, would grow up to be a serial killer.

Rachel Nickell's boyfriend André Hanscombe outside the Old Bailey after Robert Napper pleaded guilty to her manslaughter.

problem child became a monster

Psycho stalked me for months

I remember one boy holding him by the lapels and hitting him

Robert Napper is pictured growing up.

THE US RIPPER

I killed 20 vice girls

A JOBLESS loner who has confessed to the murder of at least 20 prostitutes led police to two more bodies last night.

Mummy's boy Joel Rifkin, dubbed Joel the Ripper, took officers to the remains hidden in shallow graves.

From ALLAN HALL in New York

Rifkin picked up [illegible]-a-time hookers in New York.

He says he smothered or strangled most of his victims and stored the bodies in a deep freezer in his garage before dumping them in remote areas of three states. Like Jack the Ripper, 34-year-old Rifkin allegedly butchered the vice girls he preyed on.

Police refused to comment on reports that a chain saw found at his home was used to hack up his victims for burial.

Police captain Walter Hoesch declared: "We believe him when he says he patronised prostitutes and murdered them."

Rifkin looks set to become America's worst serial killer since cannibal psycho Jeffrey Dahmer's 17-victim spree ended in 1991.

Joking

He was arrested after police tried to stop him for driving without number plates.

The bespectacled gardener led officers on a wild 20-minute chase.

A foul smell drifted from the back of the pick-up truck.

"Smells like you've got a body back there," quipped officer Sean Ruane. The joking ended when the tied-up corpse of a woman in her 20s was found under a tarpaulin.

Rifkin had never had a girlfriend. He lived with his mother Jean, 71, and sister Jan, 31, on suburban Long Island.

He says he used a wheelbarrow to cart bodies to and from the freezer then dumped them in New York State, New Jersey and Connecticut.

Late last night one body was discovered in a grave in Southampton and another in a remote area of Kennedy Airport.

LONER WITH A DEADLY SECRET: Joel Rifkin after his arrest by police

TOMORROW Screen MIRROR BRIDGET FONDA: KILLER! TOMORROW

SNAP: A Land Rover was stolen near Glastonbury, Somerset, as its owner's labrador slept in the back.

'GODDESSES' ON STANDBY

By ALAN LAW

TV Noeline is on song

US Ripper
US Ripper Joel Rifkin is arrested by police following the murder of more than 20 women.

Thursday, December 9 1999

The Mirror

EXCLUSIVE My hopes for ALL our children

EDUCATION MINISTER MARTIN McGUINNESS WRITES FOR THE MIRROR: SEE PAGES 12 & 13

BUTCHER: Smith

Beast faces quiz on 50 sex killings

By JEFF EDWARDS
Chief Crime Correspondent

A BRUTAL sex monster dubbed by police a modern Jack the Ripper was jailed for life yesterday.

Now David Smith is set to be quizzed about 50 more unsolved sex killings across Britain stretching back 20 years.

The 19-stone loner, obsessed with sado-masochistic sex, was convicted at the Old Bailey yesterday of killing 22-year-old prostitute Amanda Walker.

And it was revealed that Smith, 43, struck after being cleared of a horrific carbon copy murder six years ago because of a legal loophole.

He snatched Amanda from a London street, then raped and throttled her, mutilating her body with a knife, before dumping her body at a Surrey beauty spot.

The Recorder of London, Judge Michael Hyam, told

TURN TO PAGE 9

BUGG

David Smith
Police wanted to quiz suspect David Smith over more than 50 killings.

BIN BAG VICTIM 3

First picture of woman in Hardy triple murder case

By KANCHAN DUTT

THE ex-husband of bin bag murder victim Brigitte Cathy MacClennan spoke last night of his sadness at her terrible death.

New Zealand-born Miss MacClennan was named on Monday as the third alleged victim of murder suspect, Tony Hardy, 51.

Brigitte's family only learned of her death from TV and news reports.

Yesterday, her former husband, Jalil Amzil, 36, admitted he had not seen her for a year.

The couple had married in May, 1993 and had a child together, but divorced six years ago.

Speaking at home in Upper Holloway, north London, Mr Amzil said: "I feel sorry for her. I haven't seen her for a year – nor has our son.

"We split up about five years ago and the only relative she has here is her mum."

Mr Amzil, who remained calm but sad, added: "All I'm concerned about is the effect this will have on my children. I do not want them to find out about this - it is terrible news. It has left me deeply shocked."

Unemployed Tony Hardy, 51, has been charged with the murders of three prostitutes – Elizabeth Valad, 29, Sally Rose White, 31, and 36-year-old Miss MacClennan.

k.dutt@mirror.co.uk

SUSPECT: Tony Hardy

VICTIM: Vice-girl Elizabeth

KILLED: Mother-of-one Brigitte is third alleged victim in bin bag case

Elvis hits a record

ELVIS Presley has scored his biggest-selling album of all time, 25 years after his death.

More than eight million copies of Elvis 30 No1 Hits have been sold worldwide.

The album by the King, who would have been 68 today, has topped the charts in 25 countries.

It has spent 14 weeks in the UK charts after its September release by BMG Records.

Presley's biggest selling single is Hound Dog/Don't Be Cruel which has sold in excess of £8million to date.

BMG marketing boss Darren Henderson said: "This proves that his music is indeed timeless."

Toxic soil in protest

SURVIVORS of the 1984 Bhopal disaster yesterday dumped waste from the gas leak factory at the firm which owns the site.

Indian activists shipped seven barrels of toxic soil on the Greenpeace boat Arctic Sunrise to the Dow chemical plant, Holland.

Rashida Bi said: "We will fight on until the toxic fallout from Bhopal stops killing us."

More than 20,000 people have died since the world's worst industrial accident.

A spokesman for Dow – which bought out original owners Union Carbide in 2001 – said the protest was "regrettable". The activists were arrested.

Camden Ripper The *Daily Mirror* unmasks the Camden Ripper as Tony Hardy and shows two of his victims

Broadmoor Hospital Prison began life in the 1860s as Broadmoor Criminal Lunatic Asylum and has housed many notorious killers – including Peter Sutcliffe and Robert Napper – in the intervening 150 years.

2.00 a.m. in the morning or, on finding his mother and his "uncle" dead, he fled on his own to the door on which he knocked in the early hours. He was so traumatized that even the child himself didn't know how he got there.

Barbara Locci (nicknamed "Queen Bee" for her many extra-marital relationships) was married to Natalino's father, Stefano Mele, and lived in Lastra a Signa in the province of Florence, Italy, with her family. Her murder, along with that of her lover Lo Bianco, was the first of 16 murders of couples in cars, which would stretch across almost two decades of cold-blooded killings. The three people in the car on 21st August were returning home from the cinema when the two adults saw that the young child lay asleep in the back of the car. Knowing they had time for a sexual encounter before they made it home, Barbara's lover began removing her clothes once they parked up in a local cemetery. Before they had got very far, a lone figure appeared out of the darkness and shot them both dead with a .22 Beretta.

When Natalino Mele knocked on the door of the farmhouse where he found himself, tears were pouring down his face as he told the farmer that his mother and "uncle" – the term he used for his mother's many lovers – were dead. When police were called to the scene, they discovered eight shell casings by the vehicle, but were baffled as to who the perpetrator was or why the crime had been committed. They arrived at Natalino's family home to question his father at around 7.00 a.m. the following morning after the initial investigation had got underway. Stefano Mele agreed to accompany the detectives to the police station where he gave them a number of names of men known to have been his late wife's lovers. He seemed little surprised by the news and, having been questioned at length, was asked to return to the police station the following day. He had suggested to police that any one of his wife's lovers could have committed the crime but, on 23rd August 1968, he walked back into the police station and confessed to the killings himself. He gave a detailed description of how he and a friend, Salvatore Vinci, had seen the couple leaving the cinema and had followed them to the graveyard. He described how he was fed up with his wife's infidelities and the fact that she so openly humiliated him in front of friends and neighbours. Mele claimed that Vinci handed him a weapon and he simply killed the couple as they made out in Antonio Lo Bianco's Alfa Romeo. However, he failed to mention his son or what had happened to him.

Mele was quickly arrested and the following day police began hunting for the gun in the area where the man said he had disposed of it, but to no avail. The arrested father then changed his story and claimed he had given the gun back to his accomplice, Vinci. He then went on to retract his confession and began blaming Salvatore's brother, Francesco Vinci instead. For a number of days, Mele kept changing his story but, two years after his wife's and her lover's death, he was found guilty of their murders and was sentenced to 14 years in prison on the grounds of insanity.

By the time eight years had passed since the murders of Barbara and Antonio, Mele had spent six of those years in prison. Detectives were sure they had their man and the case was closed. Then, on 24th September 1974, detectives were called to a scene to the north of Florence where the discovery of two bodies in a parked car was made. A walker had spotted 18-year-old Stefania Pettini and 19-year-old Pasquale Gentilcore dead. Pasquale was half-naked in the driver's seat of his father's Fiat while Stefania was completely naked and found at the rear of the vehicle where her body had been posed by the killer in a spread-eagled position. Her vagina had been mutilated by a vine branch. While the young man appeared to have been shot and shell casings littered the scene, Stefania looked as though she had been stabbed multiple times. Her handbag was found in a neighbouring field while its contents had been strewn around the ground. At the post-mortem, it became clear that both victims had been shot with a .22 Beretta. The bullets proved that the young couple had been killed with exactly the same weapon as Barbara and Antonio some eight years before. But Stefania had also been stabbed at least 96 times and police were confident that it was one of the knife wounds that delivered the fatal wound to the young girl. Three men came under suspicion for the crime including Bruno Mocali, Guido Giovannini and Giuseppe Francini, although no links to the men could be found and they were all released without charge. What the police did know was that the murderer was a sexual deviant and that the first two deaths were unlikely to have been carried out by Stefano Mele. No killer was ever found.

Seven years later in early June 1981, victims five and six were discovered by an off-duty police officer out on a weekend walk with his son. Giovanni Foggi (30) was found slumped over the wheel of his car which was parked alongside a country road. He immediately called in his colleagues and they soon found the body of 21-year-old Carmela Di Nuccio lying at the bottom of a steep bank about 20 yards away from the vehicle. The lovers had died of multiple gunshot wounds from a .22 Beretta and Giovanni had been stabbed three times. Carmela's vagina had been removed by someone whom the pathologist believed had skill in using surgical instruments. The bullets were then compared to those from the 1974 killings and a ballistics match was found. Police now knew they had a serial killer on their hands. They focused their investigation on Enzo Spalletti who was renowned as an occasional voyeur and whose car had been seen in the area around the time of the murders. What was particularly interesting to police was the fact that Spalletti had seemed to know about the car and its occupants before details were released in the press. He was arrested and remanded in custody.

Just over four months later, the bodies of Susanna Cambi and her boyfriend Stefano Baldi were discovered by another young couple just north of Florence in Calenzano. The murder victims had parked their car at the scenic spot and had been brutally murdered by a cold-blooded killer who knew his victims were still alive as he inflicted the first of the vicious stab wounds they had endured. Both had also been shot. Susanna had also had her vagina removed, just like Carmela had done, but a larger area had been taken and less precision was used by the killer or killers. In addition, the victim's abdominal wall had been cut through by a single-edged knife, which was up to approximately seven centimetres long. The weapon used was a .22 Beretta and the ballistics tests proved positive as a match for the previous murders. Witnesses reported a red Alfa Romeo GT driving away at speed from the scene. The province of Florence was now alerted to the fact that in their midst lay a sadistic serial killer of young couples. Spalletti was obviously not responsible for the previous murders and he was released from jail.

Despite the fact that many locals around Florence were nervous, young couples did still hunt for isolated spots in which to make love and, on 19th June 1982, another couple – 20-year-old Antonella Migliorini and her boyfriend, 22-year-old Paolo Mainardi – were attacked by the same killer. They were close to Via Nuova Virgilio when someone came out of the bushes and started shooting at them. Antonella died almost immediately, but Paolo was able to start the car, turn on the headlights and reverse the car some distance, despite his injuries. However these, combined with the panic he must have been feeling, meant that the car ended up in a ditch and he was unable to get it out again. The killer shot out the headlights before emptying his gun into the two victims. He must have been disturbed because he didn't mutilate Antonella and instead fled from the scene and disappeared into the night after he coolly turned off the victim's engine and threw the keys into nearby weeds. He did not realize that one of his victims was still alive. Paolo wasn't able to help police, however, when he was discovered the following morning; he never regained consciousness and died from his gunshot wounds just a few hours later. The young couple had been attacked by a sex maniac nicknamed "Jack the Ripper".

In a clever move by the assistant district attorney, it was reported that Paolo was still alive when he was taken to hospital and that he'd given a clear description of his attacker to police. A man called Red Cross emergency workers following the news in the papers, at first pretending to be from the DA's office, before eventually admitting that he was the murderer. He was anxious to know what the young victim had said. Upon further investigations, police then discovered that the first two victims, Barbara and Antonio, had also been killed by the same murderer, by now dubbed "The Monster of Florence", or "Il Mostro". Police now knew that Mele could not have killed anyone since 1968, but they believed him to have an accomplice. For his part, the convicted murderer continued to claim his innocence and refused to cooperate in any of the investigations.

More than a year later on 9th September 1983, German tourists Horst Meyer and Jens Rüsch (both 24), were shot dead in their Volkswagen bus in Galluzzo. Police believe that the killer mistook the slight build of Rüsch and his long blond hair as that of a female. Then, on 29th July the following year, Claudio Stefanacci – who was 21 – and his 18-year-old girlfriend Pia Gilda Rontini were shot and stabbed in their Fiat Panda, which was parked in woodland near Vicchio di Mugello. The female victim's vagina was removed as in earlier cases although, this time, the left breast was also removed. Pia had complained to friends that she had been harassed by an unpleasant man at the bar where she worked and there were reports that the couple had been followed by a man some hours before the attack. Both victims were shot with a .22 Beretta and Pia's body had been slashed with a knife more than 100 times. It was definitely the work of the Monster of Florence, however, police still had very little to go on and no new or significant clues that would help lead them to the killer. The final murders took place in September 1985.

The two victims from Audincourt in France were on holiday in the province of Florence when they were brutally killed while sleeping in their tent. Nadine Mauriot (36) was shot and stabbed inside the tent before her left breast was removed by the killer. Her partner, 25-year-old Jean-Michel Kraveichvilli, was killed a little way from the tent where it appears he had been trying to escape his attacker. The killer, in a move not seen previously, then sent a note along with a section of Nadine's left breast to the state prosecutor to say that two more murders had taken place. The bodies had been discovered by a passer-by collecting mushrooms, just a few hours before the letter arrived.

Pietro Pacciani became of interest to police during the eight years that followed. He had already served time in prison for the murder of a travelling salesman who had had an affair with the man's fiancée in 1951. His known associates were also described as "peeping toms" with whom he was involved in an occult group. He had married and had children on his release from prison but was jailed again in 1987 for beating his wife and sexually molesting his two young daughters. He was freed in 1991.

Witnesses came forward to claim that the four men were involved in using female body parts during their satanic rituals, and

Pacciani was arrested in 1993. His trial, in 1994, was televized and became compulsive viewing, but it highlighted a complete lack of evidence in the murders. However, he was convicted of seven of the murders and sentenced to life imprisonment despite his pleas of his innocence. He was cleared by the appeal court in February 1996 after his conviction was ruled unsafe. A retrial was ordered on 12th December that same year after one of Pacciani's associates, Giancarlo Lotti, confessed that he and the former accused had perpetrated the crimes. Another of their associates was also charged with murder and, in May 1997, Mario Vanni and Lotti stood trial for five of the double murders. They were convicted and imprisoned. Police believed by this time that a gang of men were responsible for the killings. However, Pacciani never made it to the retrial planned in 1998. He was found semi-naked lying face down on the floor of his home. It was believed that he had suffered from a heart attack, however, drugs were also found in his system and police surmised that Pacciani was killed in order that the real "monster" or "monsters" escaped being brought to justice.

Police didn't close the case following the death of Pacciani and at the beginning of the 21st century made it public that they believed a group of educated, wealthy men were responsible for the murders. They released very little about the new suspects they thought responsible, although it is known that they suspected between 10 and 12 men involved in occult activities, including a doctor and an artist from Switzerland.

The Railway Ripper

1986

On 23rd May 1986, police were trying to trace bride Anne Lock, working on clues provided by viewers of the BBC's *Crimewatch*. More than 50 people phoned in after the previous night's programme. One reported that she was asked for a kiss by a man wearing one earring on a train from London's King's Cross to Brookmans Park in Hertfordshire, the same route as that used by Mrs Lock. Another said she was approached at the suburban station by a man who fled when a train pulled in. Anne Lock, 29, a secretary with London Weekend Television, vanished on Sunday evening after leaving the studios. Her husband of four weeks, 26-year-old butcher, Laurence Lock, indicated that his fears for his wife's safety were growing.

It looked rather odd when attractive bridesmaid, 29-year-old Lesley Campion, moved in with the wealthy butcher, but both denied that they were sharing anything more than their worry and grief. Lesley said: "Anne and I are best friends. I am staying with Laurence now, sharing his grief. Laurence denied that the couple were having an affair: "There is nothing between Lesley and me, and to say anything else is despicable." As he spoke, Lesley was taking messages for him at his detached home in Brookmans Park, Hatfield, in Hertfordshire. Anne, a top programme production secretary, was believed to have been kidnapped according to her husband. He was still hoping that his wife would be found alive. He had been quizzed several times by police, but strongly denied any part in his new wife's disappearance. "I know what people may say, but people around here will not be gossiping," he said. "They are good friends and know how happy we were. My wife grew up with Lesley and she has stayed with us before. She is Anne's best friend and is offering support to my wife's grandmother during Anne's absence." He said that Lesley was also comforting him. Laurence revealed that Anne could have been pregnant and that the couple were hoping for a honeymoon baby. However, the following day, Lesley packed her bags and left the Locks' luxury home, but would not explain why she was leaving. Laurence blamed "wagging tongues" for her quick departure from the house. As a nationwide hunt for missing Anne continued, baffled police were planning a dramatic new TV appeal to help them find the missing woman.

On day nine of the hunt for Anne, police asked bosses at London Weekend Television to devote their *Police 5* programme, aired on Sundays, in order to help their investigation. The request, from senior detectives still mystified by the girl's disappearance, was expected to receive a favourable hearing. As a highly-rated employee at the studios on the South Bank, it was thought that TV bosses would agree. If presenter, Shaw Taylor, got the go-ahead, it was thought that millions of viewers would tune in to watch a careful reconstruction of events. The *Mirror* presented all the known facts of the case so far on 27th May 1986 and asked for its army of readers to help police solve the riddle.

On Sunday 18th May, Anne left her home to go to work. It was about 3.00 p.m. as she cycled on her red bike to the station to catch a train. At about 8.15 p.m. she was seen leaving the studios to return home. Normally, she took the tube to Finsbury Park and then changed to a main-line train back to Brookmans Park. When she failed to arrive home, her 86-year-old grandmother, Edna Goss, who lived with the newlyweds, became worried. On voicing her concerns to Laurence, who wasn't at home, he then phoned the police.

The following day, police discovered that Anne's bicycle was missing from the shed at the station. It was found dumped in a field, still padlocked. Laurence confirmed with police that he was away on his boat with friends in Poole, Dorset, when his wife went missing. Detectives established that he was seen towing his boat with his Land Rover south of London at a petrol station the night of Anne's disappearance. On 20th May, Detective Chief Superintendent Ron Archer, head of Hertfordshire CID, told reporters that he feared for the woman's safety. The next day, Laurence Lock, having been questioned by police, strongly denied any involvement in his wife's disappearance, while a squad of more than 40 detectives became involved. On 23rd May, viewers of *Crimewatch* telephoned police after an appeal, and police revealed that there was rivalry between Anne, known as "Little Anne", and Laurence's former girlfriend known as "Big Anne". On 25th May, Lesley moved in to comfort Mrs Goss and Laurence, and Anne's colleague said: "Anne was not the sort of girl to go off on the spur of the moment. We are all worried." Three days later, the press was full of reports on how Laurence Lock had kept a bizarre rendezvous with a girl kidnap victim. He had said more than once in the days that Anne disappeared that he thought she could have been abducted, but then he told the press about how he had met a woman before his wife vanished, who had given him details about her terrifying ordeal. He said: "She was held for two weeks in a locked garage against her will. She told me she was given food and drink, then tied up and later left in a field." He then reiterated his fears for his wife when he said: "Something like that could have happened to my wife. There are some very peculiar people about." Lock called a news conference on the doorstep of his home to speak of his strange meeting, but he refused to give further details. He continued: "Someone may have seen a woman taken into a car near the studio, or a lovers' tiff." However, he declined to explain what he meant. The following day, Anne's diary was found and her husband wept as he told reporters: "I know my wife is dead. I have to accept that." He had identified her diary and telephone book which were found on 28th May in fields just a mile from their home. Police also feared the woman was dead. Detective Superintendent Ron Archer, added that no one had been ruled out of their inquiries. He confirmed that the diary was found on the banks of a dried stream, and the telephone book 500 yards away from it. Divers then commenced searching nearby lakes.

Just before the end of May 1986, Laurence Lock said he would thump anyone who asked him if it was him who had killed his wife. He cited that such a question would be "beneath contempt". But police announced that they were studying two other unsolved crimes for links to the disappearance of Anne.

Allison Day, 19, vanished in December 1985 after catching a train near her home in Hornchurch, Essex. Her body was found 17 days later in a canal in Hackney, East London. In 1983, a woman was raped after she left a train two stops before Brookmans Park.

Despite his contradictory statements to the press, which perhaps signalled his private hell, Laurence Lock hid his anguish well. He told Noreen Taylor of the *Mirror* that Anne's last words to him were: "Goodbye darling. Take care and see you soon." He believed, at this point, that the discovery of Anne's diary and telephone book meant she wouldn't be coming home but that she hadn't walked out on him either. He continued: "I had no reason to doubt her. We hadn't had a row." She wasn't hot-tempered or irrational. Jeremy Bugler, her boss at LWT described her as: "very predictable, very even-tempered. A solid, no-nonsense girl." Laurence had dismissed the information offered to detectives following the *Crimewatch* programme.

Lock's mood ranged from quiet contemplation, talking about his wife, to aggressive when questioned by other reporters, and crying when telling them how he had loved his wife. By the end of May, police believed that a cunning killer had laid a false trail to mislead them. They thought she could have been snatched as she left work in London, and not after she got off a train at her local station. However, two days later, it was known that a six-year-old boy and a taxi driver had both, independently, told police that a gunshot and screams were heard the night that Anne disappeared. The new clues, described in the press as "sensational", were given to police. Both the child and the man, not linked to the child, told police that the noises came from close to the railway station where Anne would have alighted after her journey home. The boy's evidence came to light when police were searching grass verges near the track at Brookmans Park station. Grant Banford had heard a loud bang and strange screams on the night in question, and as police searched, they were told of the incident by the boy's mother. She said: "My son called out from his bedroom complaining about the noise. I saw through the darkness a man wearing bright green trousers. It was too dark to see anything else about him, but his trousers were so bright they shone through the dark. My son keeps going on about the big bang he heard and police think it was a gunshot." Taxi boss Tim Moon also told the police that he heard a strange noise in the station at around the same time. He said: "I heard it all – a big bang and then a girl screaming. It was 9.40pm. I did not take much notice at the time because we sometimes get noises from youngsters."

In early June, detectives thought that a Sunday-night sex killer might have struck for a fifth time. They believed that the murderer of 20-year-old Helena Swann could have also killed Allison Day and 15-year-old Maartje Tamboezer. They looked at the similarities with Anne's case and that of the rape of a girl jogger some years before. Helena was attacked and strangled in her flat in West Ham, East London, on a Sunday. Allison was strangled and dumped in Hackney after a Sunday-night rail journey, and Maartje was killed near Horsley station in Surrey on a Sunday night.

On 12th June 1986, they searched the back garden of Anne's home for a disused well. Officers dashed to the house after a tip-off from a neighbour, but a 20-minute search only uncovered a manhole – which was empty. Six days later, police revealed they were searching for a man seen walking alongside a railway line late at night. He was known to have been in the area when Anne disappeared, and police launched a photofit image of the man they were looking for.

On 21st July 1987, Anne Lock was found murdered and dumped near a railway line. She had been tied up and suffocated before being hidden under bushes on the overgrown embankment 10 weeks earlier. Detectives said the killer was the same sex fiend who had murdered Maartje and Allison. Two railway workers made the grim discovery just half a mile from the spot where Anne's diary and address book were found after she disappeared. Working under powerful arc lights, detectives searched the area for clues while the body was taken away for a post-mortem examination.

Anne was threatened with a Stanley knife as she stepped off her train home, before being dragged half a mile along a remote path by the monster dubbed the Railway Killer. She was then tied up and gagged before the brutal attacker, who had already killed twice before, sexually assaulted her. He left her to die of suffocation in the bushes beside the railway. The gag was still in her mouth when she was found and the Stanley knife was discovered nearby. She had died alone and remained undiscovered for 10 weeks. Her body was so badly decomposed that it could only be identified by dental records. Police also believed the man responsible was the perpetrator of at least three rapes in the previous two years. The first was in November 1984 near Barnes Common in Southwest London, the second was in February the following year at Hadley Wood station, just two stops from where Anne met her killer, while the third was in August 1985 next to the line at West Hampstead station in North London. Detectives said the man they were looking for was white, in his mid-20s, with fair hair and an athletic build. Detective Chief Superintendent Vincent McFadden who led the hunt, said: "We are dealing with a very dangerous man who obviously has no compunction about killing." Meanwhile, more than 100 officers were drafted in to track down the monster.

Daughter of a Dutch oil executive, Maartje Tamboezer was raped and battered to death in woods near the railway line at Horsley in Surrey. She had been gagged and bound and an attempt had been made to burn her body. She was snared by her killer as she cycled along a footpath on her way to a sweet shop. She was forced to dismount by a length of cord strung across the path and made to push her bike 150 yards across a field to the woods. Secretary Allison Day alighted a train in Hackney Wick station in East London on her way from her home in Essex. She was seized from behind and choked before her body was dumped in a canal. Following Anne's murder, police throughout the Home Counties were feeding details of sex attacks throughout the area and records of known sex offenders into the National Crime Computer. Even in the early days, 90,000 fingerprints were cross-checked. McFadden said: "In all three killings there has been a tying of the hands and the use of a knife, and all took place on a footpath near a railway line."

Police then quizzed hundreds of commuters as they retraced the movements of a secretary who escaped from the railway killer after being sexually assaulted. The 22-year-old victim was ambushed at knifepoint as she walked along a footpath on her way home from work. She was saved by her mother, who found her daughter's umbrella on the path when she went to meet her. The attacker panicked after hearing the girl's name being called and fled the scene. It was the closest he had come to being caught and detectives questioned people who had travelled from London Waterloo to Oxshott in Surrey on the commuter line.

Laurence wept as he said that the killer was "a beast who must be locked up". He continued: "If anyone knows anything, they must come forward." By this time, the killer was suspected of raping 27 women across North London. Laurence accused police of "bungling" the hunt for Anne's killer. He said that police had wasted valuable time by treating him as the number one suspect and wrote to police chiefs listing their "mistakes" in the 10 weeks since his wife had died. The "Railway Ripper", as the killer was dubbed in the press, had left Anne just a short distance from her home, and the police didn't thoroughly search the area, which Mr Lock claimed he'd asked them to do countless times. In August 1986, police outlined the horrific final moments of Allison Day, and revealed that they were not searching for one man for the murder, but two. They issued a statement that said they were looking for two men seen dragging her away from a bus stop. The news was released after a dramatic breakthrough in the murder hunt. A middle-aged woman answered an appeal for witnesses on LWT's *Police 5* programme and told detectives she had seen two men taking the teenager away from the bus stop in Hackney Wick. It meant that the police were now hunting for two men in connection with the murder of Maartje and Anne. It was believed that both men were in their twenties.

On 26th November 1986, two men were quizzed over the three murders and 27 brutal knifepoint rapes. One of the men, a kung fu expert, was held for a further 24 hours in Guildford, Surrey, by police, while the second man, arrested two days after his accomplice, was questioned at length. At the same time, police threw a news blackout over their hunt for the killers. The hushed operation was imposed as a number of women arrived at Guildford police station, and it was believed that they were rape victims taking part in a series of identity parades. The women were driven to the police HQ by officers from Operation Hart, the Scotland Yard investigation into the horror attacks. The huge manhunt was launched as soon as police linked the murders of the two girls and Anne. In all three murders, the bodies had been trussed up and a knife used, and in each case, the killer had the same rare blood group. One of the men was eventually accused of the murder of a schoolgirl, a teenager and a woman in November. The 27-year-old who was also accused of three rapes appeared at Guildford Court on 1st December 1986. In June 1987, the former British Rail carpenter was sent for trial charged with the three "Railway murders" and six rapes. It seemed that the police now had the "Railway Ripper". The pictures of Anne Lock's body, badly decomposed and burnt, after the killer had set fire to it, were particularly terrible according to the prosecutor, when they were brought to trial as evidence.

The ex-wife of the man told the court in January 1988 how he could change in seconds into a "raving madman". Margaret Duffy said her husband used to tie her up for kinky sex sessions. She had feared that he was going to kill her, and even boasted to her that he had raped a girl. "The marriage was just fighting all the time," she told the court. "He wanted sex almost every night and used to force himself on me. It started off with verbal threats and then he used to hit me to make me have sex with him. He was too strong for me." The 25-year-old described John Duffy's moods as "very changeable". She added: "He could be really nice and then, without warning or reason, he could become a raving madman." Duffy, by now aged 30, was a former railway worker and carpenter who denied murdering Allison, Maartje and Anne as well as seven rapes and assaults. The last rape victim was a 14-year-old girl who was attacked just days after Duffy had been questioned and released by police earlier in the investigations. He forced the girl into a wood at knifepoint and used her clothes to bind and gag her, the jury heard. Margaret Duffy didn't once look at her former husband as she told the court about her life within their stormy marriage. The couple had married in 1980, but by 1985 it was effectively over. By then, said the prosecution, Duffy had already committed two rapes. His ex-wife told the court: "I couldn't bear to look at him or touch him. He used to lie on top of me so that I couldn't move. He would tie my hands with a belt or the cord from a dressing gown. The more I protested, the more he got aroused." She then told the court of the rape boast. "On one occasion, he was talking quite calmly for a change and he told me that he had raped a girl and that she had enjoyed it and asked him to come back for more." She continued: "He said it was all my fault. He said he took a personal stereo from her and he gave it to me as a present." In June 1985 when Margaret returned to her North London home to collect some belongings after she left her husband, she was subjected to more forced sexual intercourse. "He used to force me again to have intercourse. Once he tricked me by saying that he had baked a cake and wanted me to taste it. He told me to close my eyes and open my mouth and then he used that to stuff a hanky into my mouth and around my throat. I really thought he was going to kill me." After she found a new boyfriend, she also accused Duffy of attacking them both, and the kung fu expert used a weapon from his martial art on his ex-wife.

During the trial, Anne Lock's father-in-law collapsed outside the Old Bailey on 2nd February 1988. Mr Lock was taken to hospital as his son was inside the court giving evidence. The judge, Mr Justice Farquharson, relayed the news to Laurence Lock and halted the trial. Alfred Lock, 66, died in nearby St Bartholomew's Hospital. On 25th February, John Duffy was convicted of raping two girls aged 14 and 16. He stared blankly ahead as the guilty verdicts were read out. The older girl, by this time 19 years old, was in court to see him convicted. She had been attacked at Hadley Wood station, when it was deserted, while waiting for a train on a Sunday night. Duffy had forced her into local woods at knifepoint. The girl had told the jury:

"He said if I struggled or screamed he would slash my throat." The other victim was seized by Duffy on her way home from school near Watford in Hertfordshire. He dragged her into bushes at knifepoint, cut up her tights to bind, gag and blindfold her, before raping her against a tree. She broke down in tears as she retold her ordeal in court. He denied killing Maartje and Allison, but the judge directed the jury to find him not guilty of the murder of Anne.

On 26th February, Duffy was found guilty of the murder of Maartje and Allison and began a 30-year jail sentence. The "weedy brute" was given seven life terms at the Old Bailey after the judge branded him a "predatory animal" and told him he could well serve more than 30 years. For once, Duffy's cold, hate-filled eyes dropped to the floor. His thin face flushed, showing the spots and acne that always flared up when he was under stress. Duffy's mother Philomena and his sister Joan sobbed uncontrollably in the public gallery. He was also found guilty of five rapes. During the seven-week trial the judge ruled that there was not enough evidence to convict him of the murder of Anne. But police were convinced he was the killer. Duffy went to the cells with the stern words of Justice Farquharson ringing in his ears. "The wickedness and beastliness you caused during the murders of those two very young girls hardly bear description. Quite apart from cutting short those two young lives, you have blighted the lives of all the families of those girls. You are obviously little more than a predatory animal." He added: "You should not depend on that [the jail sentence] being the maximum." All victims of Duffy reported having been terrified of the former railway worker's "laser-beam gaze".

The Railway Ripper, as Duffy was called, had used his knowledge of rail routes and timetables to plan his attacks and make his escapes. Police were certain that the 5ft 4in martial arts fan carried out at least 20 further rapes, and dozens more victims were thought to have been too terrified by his knifepoint threats to report attacks. Duffy had moved to London with his parents when he was six years old. He'd met Margaret at an ice rink, but their marriage ended in divorce in 1986. He'd beaten his wife regularly before he turned his hatred towards other women after he discovered that he could not father a child. A Harley Street doctor told him that he had an abnormally low sperm count. As he began to single out his early victims, he came home and told Margaret: "I've just raped a girl because of you." However, Duffy hid his dark side well. He was on the management committee of a community centre a minute's walk from his council flat in Kilburn, North London. Some women even looked to his martial arts skills to protect them from muggers.

Following the trial, it transpired that Duffy killed for the first time just three months after being freed on bail by a Crown Court judge. The savage killer also slipped out of police hands a further four times before he was finally trapped. One blunder could even have led to him turning into a killer. It was reported that the "catalogue of errors followed Duffy's arrest for attacking his [then] estranged wife". He had already raped at least four times, but was not at the time under suspicion. Judge Peter Archer, a former Solicitor-General, overturned a magistrates' order remanding him in custody. Fourteen weeks after his release in 1985, Duffy raped and garrotted Allison Day. Three months later he murdered Maartje. It led to questions being raised about the handling of the case. How, after so many brushes with the law, did Duffy continue to dodge detection? Why, when police opposed bail, was Duffy allowed to walk free? The £3 million police operation launched after a string of rapes was the biggest manhunt in Britain since the search for the Yorkshire Ripper. A month after Archer granted bail for Duffy at Acton Crown Court in West London, he raped again. The killer's lawyers said the judge was told at the time that a rape allegation was being investigated, but Archer had no recollection of it whatsoever and wouldn't comment further.

Duffy then appeared on 2nd December 1985 at Hendon magistrates' court on an assault charge. The detective investigating the rape thought Duffy fitted the description given by the victim. He had taken her to the court to see the suspect, but she was unable to get a close look at him and the chance to nail Duffy was lost. Police suspected much later that Duffy may have seen the rape victim in court and decided that the police were getting too close. It was suggested that it was this near encounter that may have led him to kill. The chances are that Duffy would have progressed to killing anyway, given the facts that are known about ripper killers. Three weeks later, Allison was murdered. A month after he killed Maartje, he was arrested again when he was caught carrying a martial arts knife, however, he was once again set free.

Four days before Anne's body was discovered, Duffy was questioned by two detectives who thought he resembled an artist's impression of the killer, but it would be another four months before he was finally arrested. During that time, he claimed another 14-year-old rape victim. The two detectives reported their suspicions about Duffy to a senior officer who tried to interview him in hospital where he had taken refuge after faking loss of memory. Doctors refused to allow police to question him – Duffy, at the time the police arrived, was out watching a cricket match. He was finally arrested on 23rd November 1986 and the evidence against him was overwhelming. A search of his North London home ended his four-year reign of terror. Officers found martial arts equipment and videos, and a "rape kit", which included a bunch of more than 30 keys. Duffy claimed he could not remember what the keys were for, but he stole house keys before his attacks. Police were sure that many of the keys belonged to women too frightened to report that they had become victims of the brute. It was also thought that he kept the keys as trophies of his crimes. Detective Chief Superintendent John Hurst, the man in charge of the case, said: "There is no doubt that he carried out all these other attacks. But, we decided to charge him only with the ones where the evidence was strongest. He got his bizarre kicks from the struggles and protests of his victims. We know he pleaded not guilty just so that some of them would have to suffer in the witness box." He added: "This man is the most evil I have come across in 24 years of police work. He should never walk the streets again."

Duffy was nailed with the help of top psychologist Professor David Canter, who had been asked by police to join the hunt. His revolutionary techniques threw up just one name: John Francis Duffy. Officers were already working through a list of nearly 2,000 possible suspects, and Duffy, on file after an assault on his wife, was no. 1,596. Professor Canter from Surrey University used witnesses' statements and clues from police files to build up a profile of the killer. When his "portrait" was matched with computer records, the finger pointed at Duffy. Four months before the killer's arrest, the professor pinpointed the district in Northwest London where Duffy lived. The profile turned out to be accurate on 13 of the 17 points. It was the first live test of Canter's methods and it was so successful that police could then be trained in the new techniques. Meanwhile, John Hurst confirmed that police believed that Duffy killed Anne. He said: "We are certain that Duffy killed her. He knows it and we know it. We couldn't provide the forensic evidence to convict, but the similarities are just so startling." The fact that the body wasn't discovered for 10 weeks made it too late to gather vital forensic evidence, and the torment for Laurence Lock continued.

At the same time that Duffy was convicted, a man admitted that he had been questioned by police hunting the accomplice who was with Duffy on several of his early rapes. David Mulcahy, a close friend of Duffy, said: "they questioned me very hard but they haven't charged me so that means they have nothing on me. As far as I am concerned I am innocent." He told reporters: "I have a wife and children to look after. Do you think that I am going to talk to you about being a rapist? I knew John Duffy well but I am not going to say whether I think he is innocent or not. If the police thought I did these things then they should have charged me." At the time, police confirmed that they believed Duffy may have had two accomplices in some of his attacks. They said they knew who one of them was, but that they'd failed to get enough evidence to charge him and bring him to justice. Duffy himself was totally unwilling to help detectives and continued to feign his memory loss.

On 1st April 1988, "Ripper probe over rail rapist" was the headline in the *Mirror*. The article read: "A scruffy sex beast savagely raped a woman in a single compartment railway carriage." The details of the attack, which were revealed the previous day, were then studied by detectives hunting the Railway Ripper who had killed Debbie Linsley the week before. Debbie had also been travelling in an old-style carriage and police believed her attacker on the Orpington line to Victoria, was scruffily dressed. The latest victim, a 59-year-old, was sitting alone in her compartment, separated from other passengers by a corridor when the rapist struck. She was attacked outside Rotherham on the Nottingham to Leeds line in March 1988, but was too frightened to report it until the following month.

The rapist was described as in his twenties, about 5ft 6in tall, with black hair and a partial beard. He wore a maroon scarf and tight jeans and smelled strongly of oil and grease. By May that year, police believed they were close to trapping the Railway Ripper through a revolutionary genetic fingerprinting process. It was revealed that 26-year-old Debbie Linsley was hacked to death. She caught the 2.16 p.m. Orpington to Victoria train and was all alone in the carriage, except for her killer. Police had found traces of blood that did not belong to the victim. They then worked on the theory that the killer had been injured during the frenzied attack. His blood group was identified as a rare type shared by only a small percentage of the population. Detective Superintendent Alec Edwards, leading the murder squad, said: "This is a very significant breakthrough." Despite this, however, police remained baffled.

More than 10 years later, in March 1999, Duffy admitted to 17 more sex crimes. He was taken to the Old Bailey from prison, where he pleaded guilty to nine further rapes, six conspiracies to rape and two burglaries with intent to rape, all dating between 1975 and 1986 in the London and Hertfordshire areas. His court appearance followed interviews with police, where he also admitted to raping Anne Lock. It was also revealed that he had studied *The Anarchists' Cookbook* to find ways of silencing his victims. Police still believed that he could have been responsible for up to 50 sex assaults. His sentence was adjourned while the judge awaited psychiatric reports. It then transpired that Duffy would be giving evidence against a man who could not be named for legal reasons in a subsequent trial. On 3rd October 2000, Duffy named his childhood friend as his partner on "hunting expeditions" for women to rape and murder, a court was told. He named the man as David Mulcahy.

The two men cruised the streets in a car, clad in balaclavas, armed with a knife and playing a tape of Michael Jackson's hit song, 'Thriller'. The recording – stolen from a car – became "part of their kit", according to the prosecutor, Mark Dennis. "The tape seemed to motivate them as they sang along to the music." Dressed as joggers, they would spot a likely woman or girl, frog march her to a secluded spot and then carry out multiple assaults. Sometimes the two men would toss a coin to see which one of them would rape the victim first. Dennis added: "They called it going out hunting and they got huge pleasure and excitement out of the hunt and the waiting for victims. They would compare their latest victim with previous victims. They would feed off each other's excitement and it would encourage them to attack more." The reign of terror by the two men was carried out from October 1982 to May 1986. Mulcahy, a council plasterer, denied the three murders, seven rapes and five offences of conspiracy to rape. Duffy, however, was the chief prosecution witness against the man, who had become his childhood friend at the age of 11 on their first day at secondary school in North London. The court heard how, in their twenties, Mulcahy was a "Jack the lad" and Duffy an "introverted loner", two friends who became involved in a life of crime together. However, in 1997, Duffy spoke to police after finally deciding "to face up to his past" and start "cleansing his conscience". Referring to Mulcahy, Dennis added: "Duffy was prepared to name this defendant as his partner. In many ways, his partner was the prime mover in the three offences of murder." As mates in their young adult lives, the two men had joined martial arts classes and became hooked on kung fu videos. Although they were both married, they would go onto Hampstead Heath and frighten courting couples and gay men, while wearing Halloween masks. They would go hunting at weekends while their wives were away. Their first joint attack was in October 1982 when they seized a 21-year-old woman and took it in turns to rape her. They agreed it was "easy and exciting and they would do it again". In February 2001, the *Mirror* read: "Thriller killer and serial sex attacker David Mulcahy was caged for the rest of his life yesterday, nailed by his partner in terror." For 10 years the father of four walked the streets a free man after fellow rapist and killer Duffy was jailed for life. But Duffy dragged Mulcahy down. Haunted by nightmares and driven by self-hate, he revealed that his friend had joined him in a catalogue of 15 horrific sex crimes. Mulcahy, who said that killing made him "feel like God", was given three life sentences for the murder of the three women. He was also convicted of seven rapes and five conspiracies to rape, for which he was jailed for a total of 258 years. Old Bailey judge Michael Hyam, who was likely to urge the Home Secretary Jack Straw to impose a "full life" tariff on Mulcahy, told the killer: "There were acts of desolating wickedness in which you descended to the depths of depravity. These were sadistic killings and, of the two of you, I have no doubt it was you who derived gratification from the act." The convicted man showed no emotion as the jury returned its verdicts after deliberating for nearly 20 hours at the end of the five-month trial. There were cries of "Yes!" from the public gallery and three of his victims hugged each other. In the public gallery, Mulcahy's wife, Sandra, sat with her eldest son Gary, 22, and shook her head. Afterwards she said: "David is innocent and I will fight on to prove it." He was also to be quizzed over the unsolved sex murder of nurse Jennifer Ronaldson, aged 19, in 1980 and six other rapes in that same decade.

Police had always suspected that Mulcahy was linked to Duffy but didn't have sufficient evidence to prosecute. They also believed that he had committed further horrendous crimes since his predatory sidekick was locked up. Unsolved rapes and murders across Britain were being checked to see if there was a possibility he was involved. Feeding on each other's bloodlust – using knives, gags, tape and cloth – they subjected women to unspeakable ordeals of terror, humiliation and violence. Their predatory orgy eventually led to murder. Mulcahy was filled with loathing for women and said later: "It's the thrill you get of having power over life and death." The judge read out statements from victims outlining their ordeals in court. He said: "One speaks of nightmares and constant anxiety, off work, constant medication and therapy for years. Another says she could not comprehend how another human being could inflict such fear and terror on another. Another was quite unable to come to court, such were the devastating consequences." It hadn't just been Duffy's word that had convicted Mulcahy. There were crucial pieces of information that indicated he was telling the truth, including DNA evidence – not available beforehand – linking his accomplice to the crimes. Duffy had spent a month cataloguing everything that he and Mulcahy had done. He was even taken under tight security to where Maartje and Anne had been murdered so he could show police how the girls were kidnapped and forced to walk to their deaths. Detective Superintendent Andy Murphy remarked how taking the killer back to the murder scenes involved some "very moving moments". His astonishing U-turn involved admitting to the murder of Anne, of which he had already been cleared. As the years passed, explained the murderer, he and Mulcahy, who had found friendship at school after being bullied, developed a common lust for violence and were bound by a hatred of women. But the terror didn't stop there. When Mulcahy's son wet his bed at the age of eight, he beat him black and blue with the heavy frame of a Wendy house. He appeared in court and wept crocodile tears to gain a suspended sentence. He was appalling to the women he worked with and only ever referred to them as "fucking slags" and "sluts".

A witness said how: "One man told the other to gouge out my eyes and slice off my ears." Meanwhile the "secret hell" of one victim was revealed. A German au pair, who lost her virginity when she was raped by the killers, was known as Miss H. She was 20 at the time of the attack in 1985 and blotted out the attack for 14 years. She didn't even tell her husband when she later married. She had been raped at knifepoint as she walked home in Brent Cross, North London. She blamed herself for missing a bus home after a night out and she fled the country vowing never to return or speak English again. She was spared the ordeal of giving evidence at the Old Bailey after doctors warned she could suffer a psychological breakdown. The victim finally told her husband, and Detective Inspector Michael Freeman said: "She was one of the worst-affected victims I have met."

Jennifer Ann Ronaldson, who was raped, strangled and dumped in the River Thames, worked at Guy's Hospital in London, and was abducted and subjected to a horrific rape ordeal before she was killed. Her body was found floating in the river in November 1980 near Poplar in East London. She had a gag in her mouth and was wearing just a bra. Police strongly suspected that Mulcahy was acting alone as well as working with Duffy. There were also other attacks and it was cited that the killer committed brutal crimes. Two years after Jennifer's death in 1982, before the rape and murder spree with Duffy began, Mulcahy was questioned over an attack on a woman in East London. She picked him out in an ID parade but there was insufficient evidence to charge him. Now, however, he was behind bars for life.

Killer's Grudge

1987

A killer who stabbed a Soho vice girl to death was suspected to have had an "AIDS grudge" against sex workers, it was revealed in January 1987. Colleen Weller, 21, from Islington in North London, was found dying of knife wounds in the heart of the capital's red-light district after a ripper-style attack. Her best friend, Maxine "Sun" Payne, also 26, and herself a sex worker, said: "Since the spread of AIDS we have become targets for all sorts of weirdos. The violence has got much worse. Lots of girls around here have had knives pulled on them." The following year, in October, detectives hunting a sex fiend who murdered a sex worker, feared that he modelled himself on Jack the Ripper. The vice girl was horrifically mutilated by her killer – who might have been influenced by a then recently aired TV series on the mysterious Victorian murderer. Detective Chief Superintendent Ken Clark, who led the investigation, said: "I cannot rule out the possibility that this horrific attack may have been motivated by the programme." And, he warned sex workers: "This man could strike again. Be on your guard." The killer's victim, 31-year-old Linda Donaldson, worked in Liverpool's red-light district. Her butchered body was found in a field near the M62 motorway at Lowton, Greater Manchester. The Ripper drama, starring Michael Caine, was screened by Thames Television. A spokesman said: "There have been many books, films and TV programmes about Jack the Ripper. Our version was only the latest." He would not respond to speculation that it was a copycat killing based on the killer watching the show. The killer has never been caught.

Ripper Killer Showers at Victim's Home

1991

A Jack the Ripper-style maniac hacked a beautiful victim to death – then took a shower in her bathroom to wash off her blood, the *Mirror* reported on 3rd September 1991. The mutilated body of hospital secretary and part-time call girl Sarah Crump lay in her flat until her boyfriend let himself in after not hearing from her for several days. He found her naked body lying on her blood-soaked bed – her torso shredded by dozens of stab wounds. The 33-year-old ex-nurse had sex before she was killed, but her horrific injuries were so extensive that police couldn't tell whether she had been raped. They discovered that the maniac, who must have been drenched in Sarah's blood, took a shower after they tested heavily bloodstained tiles in the bathroom at her home in Southall, West London. A shocked police spokesman said the horror killing was "the handiwork of a most cold-blooded person who must be regarded as very dangerous." Police believed he continued hacking at Sarah's body even after she was dead. Former psychiatric patients of Sarah's were then traced for questioning. Her long-time boyfriend, a taxi driver, was released after being questioned. He had reported Lincoln-born Sarah missing after getting no answer to several phone calls and notes in the days prior to the discovery of her body. A post-mortem revealed that "fun-loving" Sarah was killed some time between a Thursday and Saturday night, just before she was found.

Just two days later, a man was arrested for the murder of call girl Sharon Hoare. The 24-year-old suspect was a VAT officer with the then Customs and Excise and was also being questioned about the attempted murder of sex worker Lucy Christopher and an another attack on vice girl Jackie Armstrong. Jackie, 25, from Earl's Court in London, helped police investigating a string of ripper-style attacks to trap the suspect. The man picked her up in the street and went to her flat for sex – then demanded cash. When she refused, he allegedly tried to strangle her, but during the struggle, a close friend arrived and fought with the attacker, punching him in the face. Meanwhile, quick-thinking Jackie went through the man's wallet – and discovered his name and address. The couple threw the man out of the flat and immediately passed his details to police at the murder incident room in Kensington – where detectives realized he lived next door to murdered Sharon, 19, and that his bedroom was separated from hers by the adjoining wall. From his windows he could have seen Sharon's comings and goings, and watched her taking clients back home. Detectives raided the home he shared with a 22-year-old girlfriend and found it empty, but four officers kept watch, two inside and two outside, and arrested him when he turned up at the flat.

Police confirmed that the man was already on a list of possible suspects before the attack on Jackie. He was expected to be charged imminently. The arrested suspect was a loner, almost unnoticed at the tiny two-bedroom apartment in Fulham. Neighbour Carl Burgess, 38, was woken by the police raid. "I could hear all this loud banging and looked out to see what was going on," he said. "My flatmate said he later saw the man being taken away in handcuffs." The massive private estate in West London was protected by a security guard in a lodge, who manned a 24-hour video monitor and automatic gates. Sharon Hoare's boyfriend was questioned twice by police about her death. Car salesman John Peacock, of Kingswood, Bristol, helped detectives voluntarily and was later arrested before being freed on bail. The trail of the ripper-style attacks began in the three weeks prior to the attack on Jackie. Lucy was hit on the head with a hammer at her flat in nearby Kensington, just a stone's throw from where Jackie lived. The sex worker then told how she fought for her life. She said that she picked the man up for "business" for £40 at Earl's Court. He suggested going back to his place ... but she thought there was something strange about him. So, she insisted on taking him back to her flat. She said: "We had sex. He let me get dressed and then attacked me. He kept saying, 'Die you whore, die you whore'." Jackie, wearing dark glasses to hide her red, swollen eyes, wept openly as she relived her nightmare. She said that suddenly he let go of her and demanded his money back. "I had the money in my pocket but I told him it was in the cupboard. He was getting really mad. I managed to get my room door open slightly and scream." Then her close friend Eustace Toussaint came bursting through the door. The man had both his hands round her throat, but he let go when Eustace came in. The friend punched the man and he fell to the floor. Jackie took the man's name and some other details from his wallet, then she and Eustace kicked him out of the flat. The events of that night meant that Jackie had to phone her mum to explain that she was a sex worker. Her mum had thought Jackie was a hairdresser, but she had turned to working in the sex trade after her father died of Parkinson's disease. "It just cracked me up. I couldn't cope and I needed the money," she said. She had given up the sex industry for three years, but returned again only after she had been kicked out of her council flat for not paying her rent. She told how less than 48 hours after the attack she was back "doing business" in order to pay her current rent. She sobbed that it wasn't easy, but that she didn't have any other alternative. She also went on to say that she had been convicted of prostitution in 1984 and in the previous 18 months had jumped bail on a similar charge.

The Customs VAT officer appeared in court on 6th September 1991 accused of the attempted murder of Jackie. Richard Heap was arrested after the spate of attacks on London sex workers, but was dramatically released on £5,000 bail on 26th September. Magistrates freed him after hearing that the sole charge against him – that of attempted murder – could be reduced after a review by the Crown Prosecution Service. He was greeted with hugs and kisses from his father and friends as he was freed, but he refused to comment as he left London's Horseferry Road Court. He was ordered to stay with his father in Reading, Berkshire, and banned from London until the next hearing. He was also suspended from his job. Meanwhile, the murder of Colleen Weller remained unsolved and it was possible that the killers were, in fact, the same man.

The Ransom Ripper

1991

The menace of a killer threatening to become the new ripper in Britain brought fear to the country's most notorious red-light district in August 1991. But, as detectives waited for his next chilling message, vice girls continued to ply their dangerous trade on the streets once stalked by the Yorkshire Ripper, Peter Sutcliffe. "I can look after myself," said Angie, a small lady who stood defiantly on her corner in the Chapeltown area of Leeds. It was also business as usual on the streets of Bradford. Angie said: "I've got a knife – a big knife – and I've got Therese, she grinned, looking sideways at the strapping young girl who shared her beat. Therese was the girl who watched out when Angie got into a stranger's car. She noted down registration numbers and checked that Angie arrived back safely. Therese had been threatened with a knife held to her throat and she knew the score.

Five weeks earlier Julie Dart, 18, had been bludgeoned to death. While she wasn't a sex worker, she was known to mix with vice girls. She was 17-year-old Angie's best friend. When the Yorkshire Ripper stalked the streets the girls were working, Angie was a seven-year-old schoolgirl, and Julie was already her friend. "She was in the class above me – we were always mates. The night she disappeared I wasn't working. Julie told me she wasn't going out so I decided not to either. I heard later she'd been trying to find me with a message.

The other girls said she'd been looking for me. She never did find me and nobody ever saw her again. I still wonder what it was she wanted to tell me." The last message received from Julie was posted to her boyfriend two days before her body was found in a Lincolnshire field. She wrote: "I have been kidnapped." By 23rd August 1991, her killer claimed he had taken another sex worker hostage. He said that she too would die unless he was paid a £140,000 ransom. He also threatened to go on a bloody rampage through red-light districts, just like Sutcliffe. Six taunting notes sent to the police by the killer were studied by handwriting experts, and he phoned to arrange a rendezvous where the ransom could be handed over. Detectives staked out the area, but the caller never showed up. Police then feared he would strike again at any time. They said they were convinced the letters were genuine. The new ripper had also threatened to firebomb stores throughout Britain. He was believed to travel extensively in the Yorkshire and West Midlands areas. In his last phone call the man named his new kidnap victim as Sarah Davis from Ipswich, but police had no record of the woman.

Among Chapeltown sex workers, there were whispers about the mystery disappearance of a girl who was often seen by the White Swan pub. One said: "All the girls are very worried about each other. We don't know if this girl has just gone off to work another area or if she is in trouble." Another woman called Jasmine thought the situation was "scary". She told reporters: "I don't get in cars with blokes any more. I try to make 'em walk home with me. But at the end of the day we ain't got much choice. We've got bills to pay like anybody else." Exactly one month later there were fears that the ripper-style killer had tried to strike again when a battered girl was found wandering half-naked in the city's streets. The 17-year-old, wearing only jeans, had severe head injuries and was said to be critically ill. The girl was attacked on the streets of Bradford, just eight miles from where Julie Dart was abducted. Police feared that the attack could have come from Julie's killer, known as the Ransom Ripper.

In January 1992, it was revealed that it appeared that Julie had been plucked from the streets and strangled by a psychopath so that he could play a "game" with police. Since Julie died the previous July, the killer had taunted police with seven letters and phone calls challenging them to find him. In one letter, he referred to the "game odds". Detective Superintendent Robert Taylor declared: "Psychologists believe this man murdered Julie to draw us into a game. The game is his core aim. He has set ground rules for something he wishes to play." Police were probing whether the "psycho" was the same man who misled officers hunting the Yorkshire Ripper more than 10 years earlier. More than 6,000 people had been interviewed over Julie's death, but the investigation was no further forward. The inquest into her death in Grantham, Lincolnshire, recorded a verdict of unlawful killing.

Between October 1991 and the new year, the police didn't hear from the killer, but within an hour of the kidnap of estate agent Stephanie Slater on 22nd January 1992, police were linking her case with Julie's murder. The following day, five senior detectives involved in the bid to rescue Stephanie sped up the M1 from the West Midlands to base themselves in the Julie Dart murder incident room. A team of West Yorkshire detectives quickly travelled the reverse route and arrived at the command centre in Nechells, Birmingham. Their suspicions were that both women had disappeared at the hands of the same man. Stephanie's ransom was collected near Barnsley, just five miles from junction 37 of the M1, which was the drop for a ransom in Julie's case. Ransom demands in both cases were made by typewritten letter and tape. From the wording of the letters, it was obvious in both cases that they had been written in advance of the kidnap and posted shortly afterwards. Trails the couriers were asked to follow were similar. Stephanie's boss, Kevin Watts, who took her £175,000 ransom to the drop-off point, followed a series of orders over a car phone to contact points where further written instructions awaited him. It was exactly the kind of trail a police courier had followed in Julie's case. The equipment and methods used to collect the money tallied. Kevin placed a holdall containing the money on a tray on a bridge parapet. The kidnapper tugged on a line and the bag literally fell in to his lap. Police believed that to collect Julie's ransom he had been planning the trick in reverse – hauling up the cash from a bridge instead of dropping it down. Both victims appeared to have been chosen at random and at the last minute. By now, the kidnap of Sarah Davis was known to be a hoax, however, when Julie's body was found, the killer sent a note to police saying: "I don't have to prove anything anymore. You know what I'm capable of now."

Stephanie had been lured by the killer to a house in Great Barr,

Birmingham, which he pretended he wanted the 25-year-old estate agent to show him around. Colleagues at the Shipways branch office saw her abductor, calling himself Bob Southwall, when he called in for house-sale particulars. The description of the middle-aged man, wearing thick-rimmed glasses and speaking with a soft northern accent, matched that of Julie's killer. Police began building a profile of the man, and re-examined past extortion attempts including one to firebomb a city centre store, which the police now knew was the Coventry connection. One of the notes demanding a ransom for Julie – that was never paid – was posted in Coventry. Her body was found wrapped in material from the Kensington Laundry, Coventry, which hadn't been in operation for 30 years. By this time, sex worker Barbara Finn, 34, and young mum, Nicola Payne, 19, were both missing and police feared the same man had abducted them, too. Police even visited the "Black Panther", Donald Neilson, in prison with regard to Stephanie's kidnap, hoping that he could provide vital clues as to the methods the killer had used. Eight days after her ordeal, Stephanie was released by her kidnapper when the ransom was paid. Police issued a photofit of the man on 5th February 1992. They also issued a vital railway badge clue, which they hoped would trap the killer. The badge, a pale blue train motif on a midnight blue background, was worn on his jacket pocket. Within hours hundreds of phone calls flooded in to police, while it was revealed that Stephanie had been blindfolded for most of her time in captivity. However, she spent several days with police in order to create the photofit. She had been driven close to her home by the kidnapper before being released, and a red Metro – also sighted near the spot where Julie's body was found – was the key, police decided. A witness was woken by the sound of the engine as the car parked in a Birmingham street. They saw a woman get out backwards from the passenger side, in a crouch. "She looked dazed ... and then ran off down the road flailing her arms like a rag doll as if trying to keep her balance," said the witness. The next day, they realized they'd seen the first few seconds of freedom for Stephanie Slater.

Stephanie was probably imprisoned in a busy workshop, detectives revealed. Throughout her horrific ordeal, the young woman could hear people moving about and their voices. She dared not cry out for fear of being killed. She was kept in a coffin inside a container. She could also hear heavy vehicles arriving twice a day, and light vehicles and trains in the distance. Police thought she could have been held in an engineering workshop or warehouse and it was believed that the kidnapper and killer was either the owner of a business or a supervisor. Assistant Chief Constable Tom Cook, leading the hunt, said: "He obviously had the keys to the building." The case featured on *Crimewatch* in late February 1992, and people were urged to come forward with any vital information. As a result, a one-legged man was arrested after a tip-off from his family. Michael Sams was held after his distinctive voice was heard on the programme during his ransom instructions to Kevin Watts, which police had recorded. His ex-wife and son-in-law contacted police after watching the TV show and 12 hours later police swooped down on his tool repair shop in a rundown area of Newark in Nottinghamshire. He was then taken to Birmingham to be quizzed by detectives. He was greeted in Birmingham by jeers from a crowd who gathered to see him, and stones were thrown at the car in which he was being transported, but his work colleagues were stunned. However, villagers where Sams lived thought he was "surly", "dour" and "odd". Meanwhile, forensic experts examined a room that Sams bought for his partner, Teena, at his workshop. Described as "a bit bigger than a cupboard and smaller than a bathroom", the room is thought to have been where Stephanie was held captive. Sams' workshop and home were quietly pulled apart by police in the search for clues and evidence. He was charged with Stephanie's kidnap on 24th February 1992. He was then driven to Leeds to be questioned about the murder of Julie. He was held on remand and later charged with the young woman's murder. In May, he was accused of attempting to extort a six-figure sum from British Rail by threatening to derail a train unless his cash demands were met. He was plagued by debt, according to former colleagues and neighbours in Peterborough, where he originally lived. By the end of the year, the SAS were called in to help police find the money Sams had received in ransom for the kidnap of Stephanie. Sixty four possible sites were pinpointed by the undercover troops and the money was found buried 20 yards from the main London to Edinburgh railway line outside Grantham, using ground-probing radar, normally used in the oil industry. The site was just two fields from the spot where Julie's body was found. Two days later, police found another substantial amount of the ransom money buried close to where the £140,000 had been found by an engineer.

In June 1993, it was revealed that Julie Dart was tied to a bed and sexually assaulted before being killed with a hammer, a court was told. Sams, however, denied he had anything to do with the girl's murder, and claimed a friend carried out the attack. By this time he had admitted to the kidnap of Stephanie. However, he admitted writing three letters to police about Julie, but claimed they had been on behalf of his friend, and denied that a letter found on his word processor which spoke of having "the best sex ever" with a Julie D, was his handiwork. Mr Justice Igor Judge asked Sams to name his friend in court, but he refused. In July 1993, Sams repeatedly wept and took great gulps of air as he told how he kidnapped Stephanie and subjected her to a horrific ordeal. He had subdued her using knives in the deserted house in Birmingham she had shown him. He chained Stephanie up for her first night in captivity, telling her that if she moved, she would bring rocks crashing down on her skull. He was given a tough examination by prosecutor, Richard Wakerley, who demanded to know why the 51-year-old was crying. Sams said he didn't know. He hadn't been crying when he built the box in which he kept Stephanie. He hadn't been crying when he put Stephanie in it, nor when he manacled her ankles, or put the gag in her mouth. He had blindfolded Stephanie as soon as he grabbed her. Sams insisted during questioning that he would only name his friend who he claimed killed Julie Dart once it was proved that he wasn't the killer. But the jury were told how Sams left 21 clues that he was in fact the murderer of Julie Dart, including that the killer was a railway "buff", documents written by the killer were found on Sams' computer, the killer used materials of the same kind found at his workshop and used buff-coloured envelopes to send his letters – the same kind found in Sams' business. There were other clues, and fibres from Sams' clothes were found stuck beneath Sellotape on the killer's letters. A typewriter bought in Sams' name was used to write a Julie ransom letter and the killer posted letters in areas that Sams was known to have visited. He was found guilty and given four life sentences on 8th July 1993. He was given life for snatching Stephanie and life for imprisoning her in a coffin for eight days. He also received life for the abduction of Julie and life for murdering her.

Stephanie was in court to hear the verdict with her father Warren. She said: "I looked at him and could not believe he was trying to play down the ordeal he had put me through. Towards the end of my captivity he pretended to be sympathetic but in court all he did was tell lies and blame everything on another man." She added that she was glad she did not know her kidnapper was Julie's murderer. Stephanie had shown remarkable courage and was praised by the judge who branded Sams as "dangerous and evil". Meanwhile, police still wanted to interview him about the disappearances of Barbara and Nicola.

The papers reported how Stephanie's courage and determination to remain calm, while duping her captor into thinking she liked him, and wanted to make friends, is probably what saved her life. Crucially she obeyed his every command, especially never to remove her blindfold in his presence. Stephanie's distress, and the fact that Sams had feelings for her, led to his downfall. He telephoned her office with ransom demands and forgot to disguise his voice. He told police he had intended to kill her, but his feelings meant he didn't go through with it. Instead, he dropped her off 100 yards from her home, because she wished to see her parents, and his Metro was spotted at the scene. By September 1993, he was trying to sell his sickening story for £10,000. It was a story he'd started writing within days of receiving his four life sentences. The *Mirror*, approached by a Birmingham news agency, rejected the offer to publish. Police and Julie Dart's distraught mother, Lynn, slammed the idea. He finally admitted to Julie's murder four days after being jailed. He had murdered her within 24 hours of kidnapping her.

In 1997, Sams snatched probation officer Julia Flack in a daring jailbreak plot. He was given another eight years to run concurrently for falsely imprisoning her. Mrs Flack fought him off when he brandished a sharp metal spike and tape to tie her up at Wakefield Prison, West Yorkshire. Michael Sams was the most difficult type of criminal for the police to combat; a cunning and ruthless "lone wolf", who would stop at nothing.

In July 1991, Sams had decided to get rich by kidnapping someone who would be valuable, and for whom a large ransom would be paid. He built a lair to keep his hostage in, then he decided on a dry run to see if his plan would work. He lured 18-year-old Julie Dart into his car and, threatening to stab her if she struggled, drove her south to Newark. There he stripped her, tied her to a chair and forced her to write a letter to her fiancé asking for money to be paid for her release. He then pushed her into a cell he had constructed out of timber and metal sheets. Sams went home, but his phone rang that night, alerting him to the fact that Dart had escaped. He had rigged up a trigger mechanism, which meant an escape from her cell would cause his phone to ring. Julie had smashed her way out of the cell, but there was no way out of the workshop for her. Sams rushed back to the scene and murdered Dart with a hammer. He wrapped her body in old sheets and blankets, and, the next night, put her body in the boot of his car and drove to a country lane near Huntingdon to dump her body in a field. Her letter had arrived with her family who had called in the police. But a bombshell was to follow. Even though his victim was dead, Sams sent a letter to the police demanding £140,000 for Julie's safe return. He demanded a bizarre communication chain using the personal columns of a newspaper. However, when Julie's body was discovered, he abandoned his extortion attempt. Sams' plan had not worked the way it was supposed to have, but as far as he was concerned, it just needed fine-tuning. He needed another hostage. In January 1992, he struck again when he kidnapped Stephanie. It had been her first appointment of the day. By lunchtime, she had not come back to her office, and her colleagues had begun to worry. When the phone rang at 12.22 p.m., their anxiety turned to terror. A man's voice told receptionist Sylvia Baker: "Stephanie's been kidnapped. A ransom demand will be in the post tomorrow. If you contact police, she will die." At the house, Sams had held a knife to Stephanie's throat, then bundled her into a car and drove her to the same lair where he had kept Julie. This time he had refined his plan by constructing an escape-proof cell – a wheelie bin with a lockable lid. After forcing Stephanie to strip naked, she was pushed inside the bin and the lid locked. The ransom demand was soon received. The deadline was set for 29th January. If the money was paid she would be released unharmed two days later. If not, she would die. Chillingly, the package had included a cassette tape with Julie's faltering voice begging the police to cooperate with her kidnapper. On 28th January the phone rang at Stephanie's office and Sams demanded to speak to her boss, Kevin Watts. When Watts answered, Sams asked: "Have you got the money ready?" Told that he had, Sams snapped: "You will get a call at three o'clock tomorrow" and promptly hung up. Police were secretly recording the call. It proved a vital breakthrough. In the meantime, the money was assembled. When the call came the next day, Kevin Watts was ordered by Sams to drive to Glossop near Manchester. It was the start of a trail of clues left by the kidnapper that eventually led Watts with the bag of money to a bridge over a disused railway in the Pennines, near Barnsley. In the misty darkness Watts saw a tin tray on the bridge parapet. As instructed he placed the cash on the tray. Down below, hiding in the pitch dark, Sams tugged a rope and the money fell at his feet. He jumped on a motorbike and escaped. Although Watts had been shadowed by scores of undercover police, Sams had got away with the money. The bag with a radio tracker in it was still on top of the bridge. At his lair he opened the bin and told Stephanie: "I've got the money, you're going home". Sams was true to his word. After blindfolding her, he drove her to the end of her street in Birmingham, and let her go. He thought he'd got away with it, but with Stephanie free, the media had the story and the hue and cry unnerved him. He rang her office and threatened receptionist Sylvia Baker, not knowing that the police had left their tape recorder in place. On 20th February the tapes were played on *Crimewatch*. It was the beginning of the end for Sams.

Russian Rippers

1992

A sex killer known as Russia's Jack the Ripper was sentenced to death for two murders and nine rapes on 30th April 1992. Alexander Timofeyev, a 37-year-old shepherd, was said to have claimed he went berserk when he heard the clatter of women's high-heeled shoes. He was to be shot. A Russian newspaper said that the killer's last words to the court in Pskov were to blame the "Bolsheviks and democrats for not taking care of the working people". His crimes first came to light in the summer of 1990, at a time when the Russian press were only just beginning to sensationalize ripper killings and serial killers. Timofeyev had protested his innocence throughout the six-week trial, even though a number of women gave evidence that he had raped them. He was arrested when he was found threatening a woman with a knife in her apartment building. At the same time, the trial of Russia's notorious ripper killer, Andrei Chikatilo, continued.

Born in the Ukraine just before the Second World War, not long after a terrible famine that blighted the country, Chikatilo was repeatedly told the story that his older brother was murdered and eaten by the neighbours. Whether he even had a brother is questionable, but this is the tale he was told over and over again by his mother. Food had been desperately scarce and the story became ingrained in his memory. Whether it was this that fuelled his hatred and loathing years later is undecided, but he was to become one of Russia's most feared ripper killers. He was finally caught and eventually convicted of 53 murders on 14th October 1992.

He married and he and his wife had two children, despite his impotence, and Chikatilo worked as a teacher. He was good at his job, but was accused of molestation of a number of children he taught in March 1981. His life fell apart and he moved his family to Shakhty, where they could start again. However, he soon turned to vicious ripper killings, when he discovered the sexual release that killing gave him. His first victim was a nine-year-old girl whom he had intended to rape, however, when he was sexually unable to perform, he stabbed the little girl to death in a violent, sadistic attack. He found himself ejaculating as he thrust the knife into the tiny child, which led to one of the most horrific ripper cases of all time. Knives and other sharp and deadly weapons became his surrogate penis and boys, girls and women were not safe from his heinous attacks. Victims were lured to a rundown shack which the killer bought, where he thought he was safe from detection, but police were soon under no illusion that they were looking for a ripper killer, a serial killer of the most dangerous and violent kind. He was dubbed the Rostov Ripper. He was a cannibal, also dubbed the real-life Hannibal Lecter in the press when he gave a sinister smile when found guilty of his crimes. The evil grandfather had literally slaughtered 21 boys, 14 girls and 17 women in Russia. His reign of terror had lasted 12 years, and while some victims were raped, others were mutilated and eaten. His victims' families who were forced to hear the

330-page verdict screamed for his blood as the bulging-eyed killer sat in a white metal cage in the courtroom. One woman shouted: "Let me tear him apart with my hands". Relatives had wept when they heard how Chikatilo cut out hearts, stomachs and tongues, and gouged out eyes while his victims were still alive. Chikatilo tried to show he was mad, but psychiatrists said he was sane. He was caught after the biggest manhunt in Soviet history – one which was littered with blunders. Three other suspects were arrested and one was actually executed for one of the ripper murders. A second suspect tragically killed himself. At one stage, police actually arrested Chikatilo, but didn't think he was the man they were looking for, so the ripper killer was freed and able to kill again. However, he eventually confessed to the murders of 56 people. Only the bodies of 53 of his victims were found and he was convicted of their murders and sentenced to death. He was executed on 14th February 1994 by firing squad.

Robert Napper

1992

A battered toddler was struck dumb with fear on 15th July 1992 after seeing a sex fiend slash the throat of his young mother. Alex Nickell, aged two, was viciously beaten by the maniac who molested and murdered his mum, Rachel, in broad daylight. He was found clinging to her half-naked body, caked in mud and blood and with his T-shirt ripped from his back. Police, shocked by the savagery of the murder, were desperate to talk to the small child, who almost certainly held vital clues. But he had been unable to utter a word since the 10.00 a.m. killing of his mother on London's Wimbledon Common. Rachel Nickell, 23, from Balham in South London, was ambushed as she walked through a wooded area of the common with Alex and their pet dog Molly. One theory at the time was that the curly-haired boy was grabbed and dragged into undergrowth by the crazed ripper killer as bait. When Rachel followed she was ferociously attacked. Her jeans were pulled down and she was severely sexually assaulted before being repeatedly stabbed and her throat cut. The terrified little boy clung to her body for 40 minutes before they were seen by an elderly walker. At first he thought Rachel was lying down to cool off in the shade, before he realized the horror of what he'd stumbled on. Alex was taken to hospital for treatment. He was comforted by his father, André Hanscombe. Police confirmed that they would make no move to interview the child until given the all-clear by a psychologist. Detective Chief Superintendent John Bassett, who led the murder hunt, said the killing was "frenzied". He added: "The boy himself had been subjected to quite a vicious assault. He had been physically beaten." A shocked senior detective described the murder as: "The worst I have ever seen". Chief Inspector Michael Wickerson was called to woodland – where the child was left clinging to his butchered mother. Mr Wickerson said: "The sheer ferocity of the attack on an innocent, unsuspecting woman, walking in one of the nicest parts of London, is absolutely horrendous. I have never seen anything so bad. The boy was clinging tightly to the body. He was simply cuddling his mummy. The child was covered in blood and dirt." A man was spotted washing his hands in a nearby stream following the attack. Rachel's throat had been savagely cut to prevent her screaming for help. But broken oak tree branches and flattened undergrowth showed that Rachel had put up a tremendous struggle. An elderly man made the gruesome discovery around 10.40 a.m. in the shadow of the famous Windmill landmark – a popular meeting place. He scooped up Alex and rushed to the clubhouse of the London Scottish Golf Club to raise the alarm. Rachel's dog was found wandering nearby. The murdered mother, who was described as "lovely", had left her car in a nearby car park. Rachel had strolled into the woodland keeping an eye on her son. She was attacked just 200 yards from her car. It seemed evident that Alex had been dragged along the ground. Golfers teeing-off were ordered back to the car park to stand by their vehicles, it was then that Rachel's 12-year-old Volvo was identified. It was the only car without a driver. Police immediately traced the registration number and there was an address on the dog's collar. There were reports of two men seen at different times running away from the murder scene. One was described as blond with a ponytail and in his twenties, while the other man was wearing a white T-shirt and jeans. The 1,100 acre site, popular with joggers and dog walkers, was often plagued by flashers. At all times, there were six rangers on duty, three on horseback and three on foot. It was estimated that up to 100 people would have been in the area at the time. A special police unit began an inch-by-inch search of the area for the murder weapon. Scotland Yard issued a warning to women to avoid secluded spots on the common, and parents of local children were told to be on their guard.

It was reported in the papers that Alex could face a lifetime of torment unless he received immediate help. It was noted that what he had suffered would have a profound affect on him, while other experts disagreed and thought his young mind would be able to "wipe out" the horrific ordeal he had witnessed. Meanwhile, the shattered boyfriend of Rachel, André, asked how anyone could be so savage in their attack. He made a plea that anyone with any information should come forward before the killer could destroy another life. In the days following the murder, friends spoke lovingly about the "marvellous mother" who had been tragically killed. One friend said: "Rachel was one of those people who brought out the best in others", while another said she was "one of the loveliest and most beautiful women I've ever laid eyes on". Rachel was beautiful, fit, and was keen on aerobics, jogging and swimming. She was a devoted mother who cared for others. Those she left behind were completely devastated.

Rachel now lay in a hospital mortuary. She had been repeatedly stabbed and the frenzied killer had used a six-inch sheath knife to cut her throat. An imprint of the blade's brass hilt had been left on the victim's flesh. Alex began to talk again in the days following the attack, but he didn't utter a single word about what he'd witnessed on Wimbledon Common. But, while the country was in shock at the brutal murder, Canadian Mounties were helping to trace Rachel's parents who did not yet know of their daughter's death. They had flown to North America a short time before to see the Great Lakes.

Police meanwhile revealed that they had two vital clues to Rachel's killer. Rachel had scratched the murderer in her desperate struggle to fight him off. Skin and body tissue found under her fingernails was examined and a size 10 bootprint was found in the mud near her body. It was thought the killer was around 6ft tall and weighed 13 stone. Police were also considering the fact that Rachel might have had a stalker because she regularly walked on the common. Later in July, André and Alex returned to the spot where Rachel was found along with a lookalike friend who was going to help police stage a reconstruction of the killing. The trip, however, proved too much for her and she fled the woods in tears after laying a single red rose where the ex-model was discovered. By this time, police had found three knives, but none was the murder weapon. On 2nd August 1992, a thousand people marched in silence to the scene of Rachel's murder and wept at an emotional tribute from André. His words, about her "savage and brutal" killing, were read out by a family friend, Gordon Hammond. The crowd laid wreaths and flowers.

On 10th August, police arrested a former undertaker at his flat. The 26-year-old was also questioned about the murder of 19-year-old Katie Rackliff, who was also stabbed repeatedly and sexually assaulted six weeks before in Cove, Hampshire. Police swooped on the suspect's home in Toxteth, Liverpool, but they were also planning raids on five London addresses. The Liverpool suspect was driven to London and detectives hoped that the arrest would bring their 25-day hunt for Rachel's killer to an end. Both Rachel and Katie had been stabbed with such force that ribs were broken. Simon Murrell, the main suspect at the time, was often known to stay with his sister in Sutton (formerly in Surrey, now Greater London), but emotions were running high when he was brought to London and police refused to say where he was being held. Police refused to say whether Alex, who had just turned three, would be present at an identity parade, while searches were carried out at addresses in Sutton, Wimbledon and Tooting in South London. Murrell was released by police after questioning, but then immediately arrested on a charge of rape in Liverpool in 1991. He had been the 13th man questioned over Rachel's killing. Then, in September 1992, Colin Stagg, 29, a newspaper delivery man was charged with a sex offence on Wimbledon Common. Stagg, from Roehampton, South London, appeared before magistrates on the 21st of that month. He was accused of indecent exposure on a playing field, while another man was being held by detectives investigating the murder. He had been arrested at his home after the screening of a videofit picture of a suspect was shown on *Crimewatch*.

The inquest in February 1993 into Rachel's death heard how she had been stabbed 49 times. Meanwhile André made plans to leave for France with his young son. It was something that he and Rachel had dreamed of doing before her young life was tragically cut short. With the killer still free there were fears for Alex. Westminster Coroner's Court was told how Rachel had fought desperately for her life, but she was knifed in the heart, lungs and liver. One hand was slashed as she tried to ward off the savage blows. Even after she was dead the frenzied attack continued.

Rachel and André had met when she was a swimming pool lifeguard. That fateful morning André said goodbye at their home in Tooting as he set off for work as a dispatch rider, while Rachel headed with Alex and Molly for Wimbledon Common. In a quiet voice, André told the coroner Dr Paul Knapman: "She had been to Clapham, Tooting and Wandsworth Commons, but changed to Wimbledon because it seemed it would be safer." Rachel was seen alive at 10.20 a.m. by actor Roger McKern as he cycled to work. "She had stopped and she was looking back for her child to catch up with her," he said. The inquest was told how she was found by retired architect, Michael Murray, as he walked his dog. Mr Murray told the inquest that he released Alex's tight grip on his mother's arm and picked him up and ran off to get help. "There was no sign of life. There was no flow of blood from her wounds. Her skin had an unnatural pallor so I concluded she was sadly dead." Recording a verdict of unlawful killing, the coroner described it as "a truly horrific story". He added: "I hope the members of the family may begin to rebuild their lives." For André, the inquest could not end soon enough. When the coroner gently asked about his plans for the future, it was all he could do to tell of a move abroad. It was Rachel's father, Andrew, who spoke to reporters. Andrew and his wife Monica, alongside André, had played a vital role in coaxing Alex back to recovery. For the previous six months they had joined in therapy sessions with psychiatrists in the hope that the youngster might be able to talk about his mother's death. From being unable to leave his father's side, Alex had progressed to the point where he could spend a night with his grandparents. The tragedy had clearly torn the family apart. "You can never go back to life as it was before," said Mr Nickell. "Things have gone and they cannot be replaced. Life is never normal again. We survive from day to day." At this point it was believed by police that 15 to 20 people on the common that day had still not come forward. Mr Nickell made a plea for them to talk to police. John Bassett, the man still leading the hunt, was convinced that the man seen washing his hands was the suspect he was looking for. He spoke of his deep regret that the maniac was still at large. Six thousand names were fed into the police computer with regard to the murder and 300 of them had been extensively questioned. Mr Bassett was fairly sure he'd know the man when he was sat across a desk from him. Unfortunately, there were few hard facts for the

30-strong team of detectives to go on. All they had was that their man was white, aged between 27 and 30 and wore a white top and jeans. Mr Bassett had built up quite a comprehensive picture of the suspect. It was believed that he was unemployed, didn't have a car, but may have had a bike. He lacked self-esteem and was probably haunted by feelings of sexual inadequacy. "Someone you would barely notice, and someone who resents that anonymity." He said: "I know this man lives within a couple of miles of the common. There would be no reason for him to travel to commit a random attack or a murder. He was probably a flasher, someone who hung around watching attractive women. Obviously he fantasised about someone blonde and beautiful like Rachel. And unfortunately for her, there she was on the bridle path in the wrong place at the wrong time ... She had been pestered by men in other places. And, we know she was able to coin the sort of clever brush-off that would make a man like him feel even less of one. Perhaps it was something she said when he approached that turned his intention to rape into murder." However, a year after the murder it was suggested that the maniac may have been after her son and that Rachel died trying to protect him. This was the new theory for a time after detectives questioned the child. Monica Nickell said: "All we know is that he said he was grabbed first and then the man attacked mummy." Mrs Nickell said that the family had hoped that Alex hadn't really seen anything, but they learned after gentle questioning by police that he had, in fact, seen everything.

Jobless Colin Stagg was charged with Rachel's murder on 17th

August 1993. He was arrested after a four-month undercover operation by police and a policewoman who befriended him. The 30-year-old had a series of secret dates with the woman detective who had volunteered to help in the hunt for the knifeman. He was taken to Wimbledon station for questioning and was later formally charged. He was charged with a crime that had shocked the nation, and "rocked Britain to its roots". On the anniversary of Rachel's death, Stagg had complained that he was being "hounded" by detectives. He said: "The police are convinced I did it because I am into witchcraft and have painted by bedroom black. But I am innocent. Whoever did it is a nutter and must be caught before he does it again."

In November 1993, the bodies of a mother and her four-year-old daughter were found brutally murdered in their basement flat. The woman had been stabbed in the stomach and her little girl was suffocated to death. Police broke into the flat in Plumstead, Southeast London after a worried neighbour dialled 999. Officers were visibly shaken by the murder scene. A man was arrested nearby and was quizzed by police. A Scotland Yard spokesman said: "We are treating this as a murder inquiry. It was a very brutal and savage attack on a defenceless young mother and her daughter. We are questioning a man about the deaths but we are appealing for witnesses." It led to a hunt for manic "ripper". Samantha Bisset, 27, was butchered in a frenzied attack at her home and her daughter Jazmine was smothered in her bed. The police described the murders as horrific. Samantha had been so badly mutilated that it was very difficult to tell if she had put up a fight or not. One detective said that she had been stabbed, ripped and cut again and again. She had been stabbed 70 times with a seven-inch blade. Samatha's boyfriend and another man, Jazmine's father, were both eliminated from inquiries. Meanwhile police warned of a "lonely hearts" danger. It later transpired that four-year-old Jazmine had been sexually assaulted before she was suffocated. It was known that Samantha had used contact magazines. Police said: "Some people using dating services are very strange and anyone arranging dates should be very careful."

In September 1994, Colin Stagg was freed after being dramatically cleared of Rachel's murder. It was reported he might be entitled to a £60,000 payout. Stagg was acquitted after the judge rejected evidence from the undercover operation to trap him. Hours after walking from the Old Bailey, he started the scheme for a financial payout by touting his story for £50,000 and he hoped to win at least £10,000 compensation for the year he spent in prison since his arrest the summer before. The eight-day Old Bailey hearing involving complex legal argument saw Stagg freed by Mr Justice Ognall. Stagg then vowed to "sue the arses" off the police and stated he would take out a separate action against Dr Paul Britton, a psychologist who helped police. Stagg was expected to issue civil proceedings for malicious prosecution and false imprisonment, however, he would have to prove that the police and the psychologist went out of their way to implicate him.

In October 1994, the police started again and put a new squad in place to try to nail the murderer, after the murder case against Stagg was thrown out of court. Twenty officers, including some who took part in the original investigation, aimed to interview witnesses and study the evidence again. Exactly a year later, the ripper who stabbed and horrifically mutilated Samantha and then sexually abused and murdered her daughter was sent to Broadmoor on 10th October. Robert Napper dramatically changed his plea in court and finally admitted killing Samantha and Jazmine, as well as sex attacks on three other women. He had denied murder when the Old Bailey trial started the week before, but the judge ordered an investigation into whether he was sane enough to be tried. Five psychiatrists decided he was a paranoid schizophrenic and Napper pleaded guilty to manslaughter on the grounds of diminished responsibility. Napper, 30, got into Samantha's flat in Plumstead and sexually abused her, stabbed her eight times in the neck with a lock knife and then mutilated her body – even keeping part of her abdomen as a gruesome trophy. Napper's reign of terror had begun in March 1992 when he beat up and tried to rape a 17-year-old girl as she walked home alone in Hither Green, London. Eight days later he threatened another 17-year-old at knifepoint and tried to rape her as she took a short cut across fields in Eltham, London. Two months later he beat up and raped a 22-year-old mum as she pushed her two-year-old daughter in a buggy on the same path, the court heard. Napper was sent to Broadmoor for an indefinite period after doctors said he was "highly dangerous and posed a grave and immediate risk to the public". One said he should be detained "for many years".

Even his lawyer described him as a "grossly psychotic and ill man". Detective Superintendent Michael Banks said later that the murders were among the worst cases of his 30-year career. A woman police photographer who pictured the scenes was so shocked she hadn't worked since. Samantha's mother, Maggie, 53, collapsed and died just two days before Napper's court confession. Her husband, 61-year-old Jack Morrison, said that as far as he was concerned Napper effectively killed his wife too. The ripper killer was then to be interviewed by police in connection with Rachel's murder.

In 2008, it was revealed that police had missed six chances to nail Robert Napper for the murder of Rachel. The ripper had been on a rampage of sex attacks in parks and commons around Southeast London. He confessed to rape in 1989, three years before he stabbed Rachel to death in front of her son. But incredibly it wasn't followed up. Met police chief John Yates, apologized for the blunders in December 2008 and admitted: "Had more been done, we could have prevented this." If Napper had been stopped when he should have been, Rachel would never have met him. His DNA was on file but they still failed to follow up the rape, then after Rachel's death, he was named as suspect in a string of attacks across Southeast London, known as the Green Chain rapes. It was thought that he carried out 106 sex attacks over a five-year period. It was the killing of Samantha and her daughter that finally trapped him. He then admitted, much later, to killing Rachel. He was sentenced to "indefinite detention" in Broadmoor. At Napper's court appearance were Rachel's parents and her boyfriend, André, who did not speak to each other, having fallen out since Rachel's death. A neighbour of Napper's had named him as the Green Chain rapist, but the murderer refused to give a blood sample and the police never followed it up. Rachel's case was reopened in 2001 when DNA advances showed samples on her body matched Napper. In addition, flakes of red paint found in Alex's hair matched those on a toolbox at the killer's house.

Napper told his mother in September 1989 that he'd raped a woman on Plumstead Common. She told police who could find no record of the attack. In fact it was in a house which backed onto the common. They had a DNA sample that could have nailed him in days. In 1992, Napper was named as matching the Green Chain rapist, wanted for more than 100 attacks. He deliberately missed his blood test appointment and it was never followed up. In October that year he was arrested for trying to obtain official police notepaper. Police found knives, a .22 pistol and crossbow, and a diary, but didn't reassess him as the rape suspect. Police failed to link the murders of Rachel, Samantha and Jazmine earlier because they were focused on Colin Stagg.

Napper had been "a strange kid that nobody liked", at school. One former student said: "He was weak and feeble with greasy hair and spots. He had no mates and would just lurk around on his own at break times." He was ruthlessly bullied by other kids who would sing while kicking him in the head as he lay on the ground. It happened regularly, and wasn't helped by his troubled home life, where his parents often had violent rows. He underwent a chilling transformation that saw his mother Pauline – who destroyed all photos of him – declare after his conviction: "I had my worries but I never knew he'd turn out how he did. If he ever walks out I will be waiting for him myself because he won't walk away alive. He should die a slow death and be treated in the same way he treated those poor people." The signs that he was disturbingly different began to surface from an early age. He was still at school when his mum grew so alarmed at his behaviour that she had him seen by a shrink. When he got home he grinned mirthlessly at his father: "The psychiatrist thinks I'm mad, Dad." It was a diagnosis that would prove chillingly accurate. In his early teens he was diagnosed with Asperger's Syndrome, he was disturbed and reclusive. He bullied his younger brother Steven as his schizophrenia grew worse. His bedroom was obsessively tidy and he began spying on his sister Gillian as she undressed. He became increasingly violent and even shot his own brother in the face with an airgun. He was later fined for carrying the weapon in public. He began working at a plastics factory in Thamesmead and trawled the miles of footpaths linking local paths and commons, called the Green Chain. He began stalking women, flashing at them, and was also a peeping tom. His sex attacks began in earnest in 1989, and on one occasion he forced an 18-year-old girl to strip in a field before he stabbed her in the breast. After the police began linking their investigations, Napper simply switched his activities to another part of London. A mum stalked by Napper a year after he killed Rachel said she was "so lucky to be alive". Then aged 26 she was targeted by the killer for months before he climbed on to a wall by her open bedroom window. She was saved by a neighbour who saw him lurking and called police. Speaking about her escape, the woman said: "It sends a shiver down my spine when I see how organised he was, with maps and plans and places to spy on women. Who knows how many times he'd followed me or looked in on me." The woman, who didn't wish to be identified, was living in a flat backing on to Bostall Woods. She said: "It was a hot summer and my daughter was six months old. I would often leave curtains and windows open in the bedrooms as I tried to get her to sleep. I would wear crop tops and cut-off shorts. In the privacy of my own home I don't think I was doing anything wrong. There was a noise in the garden one evening and I heard a neighbour shout and my husband rush out. A man ran across the garden and police arrived shortly afterwards." Two officers stopped Napper, then 27, at the end of the road, but took no action after he claimed he was "going for a walk". Months before he was caught at the woman's home, Napper had stalked her as she walked her three German Shepherds with a friend. She recalled: "The dogs started to act strangely. Then I heard my friend shout, heard rustling and saw someone run out of the bushes." She was confident it was Napper. After Samantha and Jazmine were killed, the blonde woman had no choice but to move to Kent after detectives warned her she could be a target as she was the exact profile the killer was looking for.

Thirteen years after he was sent to Broadmoor, Napper learned that his grim cell would be his home until the day he dies. His fellow inmates include Peter Sutcliffe and Robert Maudsley, who ate part of the brain of one of his four murder victims. He was charged in 2007 with Rachel's murder, while incarcerated at the secure hospital. One of the other inmates who wanted to kill Napper was Wayne Campbell, who murdered his 17-month-old daughter Daniella by stabbing her in the face. In 2008 it was reported that Napper remained deluded. At the Old Bailey trial into Rachel's killing the court heard how Napper believed he had a Master's degree in maths, had won the Nobel Peace Prize and been awarded medals for fighting in Angola and had millions stashed in a bank in Sidcup, Kent. He also believed his fingers had been blown off by an IRA parcel bomb but had miraculously grown back. He was convicted and kept under close watch. He had a particularly specific *modus operandi* and was a blitz attacker, stabbing his victims – all women who were unknown to him – many, many times. It is also believed that he killed Claire Tiltman, 16, and Jean Bradley, 47, both in 1993. The fact that he killed women in front of their children was cited as rare, but experts thought he probably did this because he knew that a mother was less likely to fight back or to flee if she thought her child could be harmed. Tragically the MO of this ripper killer led to many families being torn apart and children left to grow up without their mothers. "I saw a knife, then blood ... I knew she was dead." Alex Hanscombe broke his 18-year silence over his mother's death in January 2011. "The memories are hazy now ... but they still sometimes come. And the horrifying images will never go away."

"After 18 years Alex is finally ready to speak publicly about one of Britain's most disturbing murder inquiries, solved a number of years after Rachel Nickell's death. In a dignified, calm voice – free of any bitterness, self-pity or tears – he re-lives the day he lost his mother and his life changed forever. He is back on Wimbledon Common in South West London that July morning in 1992, walking with his mother and their dog, Molly. He sees the man, tall and slim with brown hair, appear out of nowhere, before he's knocked to the ground. Then the flash of a knife blade and the blows raining down on his mother, until the man flees. He pictures the bank notes which have fallen from his mother's pocket. He picks them up and tries to give them back to her, placing one on her forehead. He sees blood and, even though he is a toddler, he is aware she is never coming back.

"Suddenly, he is surrounded by the concerned faces of adults. Police arrive and he is placed in an ambulance and given a sedative, waking later that afternoon in hospital to see his father André crying. 'I was only a small child, but I knew she was dead,' he said. 'I wasn't frightened, there was no time to be scared. I just remember the shock of knowing my mother was gone for ever.' Alex has lived almost all of his life with the memory of what he witnessed when his 23-year-old mother was stabbed 49 times and sexually assaulted by the man who would much later be identified as paranoid schizophrenic and serial rapist Robert Napper.

"Napper was finally convicted of Rachel's death, the verdict being manslaughter on the grounds of diminished responsibility. For many years, his mother's killer featured in Alex's nightmares, but he could tell no one. Not the police, not the child psychologists, not even his father. So it is perhaps a sign of his new maturity – following a troubled, angry adolescence – that he feels able to give his first interview about his mother's killing. He knows that, for many, he will always be the 'tragic tot' found by a passer-by, covered in blood, clinging to his mother, crying 'Get up, Mummy' – even though that isn't part of Alex's memory. Few could believe that such a child could ever be happy again. But he has a girlfriend, Alba, a 20-year-old student. He is a talented guitarist and has studied at music school, including a spell in London.

"He would certainly look the part of the rock star with his flowing mane of dark, curly hair and cool, laid-back air. People are always telling him he inherited the heart-melting smile of his mother, a former model. Above all, he wants those people who worried about him as a child, who sent him letters and presents, to see that 'something positive can emerge from something negative'.

"'I forgave the person who killed my mother long before I even knew who it was,' he said. 'Until you forgive, you can never move on with your life. I don't feel damaged by what happened. I had my mum for the first few years of my life – the most important ones – and being angry or upset isn't the way to go.' After his mother's death, Alex was taken to France by his father, André, to escape the 'goldfish bowl' of attention and moved again three years later to a village in Spain, where he has since enjoyed a normal life.

"Alex credits André with giving him the security and protection he needed – although he admits that, during his childhood, he took out much of his anger on him. 'I'm grateful to my father for taking me abroad to live when I was small, so I could grow up without the tag of being Rachel Nickell's son,' he said. 'If I had stayed in Britain I think it might have been a different story. I have never been back to Wimbledon Common and I don't visit my mother's grave. I'm not someone who broods on the past. We have pictures of my mother around the home, but it is not a shrine. I have never read any books about the case, though I am aware of all the official documentation. Anyway, I don't need to know anyone else's version – I saw what happened. You don't remember everything from when you are small, but you remember the big things, those that change your life. I clearly remember walking in the park with my mother and Molly and being pushed over by a man, who then attacked my mother. I knew something bad was happening. I saw the knife in his hand and when I saw her lying on the ground covered in blood, I realised the consequences. When I woke up in the hospital the next day, I remembered everything. I didn't ask for my mother once.'

"All Alex can remember of his mother, apart from that final day, is her warm, loving presence. But his dad has told him they were so close they were like interlocking circles. André was so convinced Alex wouldn't want to live without his mother that, in his grief, he considered killing himself and his son.

"Holding little Alex, who had lost the confidence to walk after what he had witnessed, André asked his son if he wanted to go on. Astonishingly, Alex says that, despite his young age, he remembers and understood clearly what his father was saying.

"'I remember saying, "Yes, I want to go on". I understood what he was asking me. But I have never wanted to die or end my life, no matter how difficult it might be. People think that when something like this happens, it's the incident that matters, but the biggest challenge is what happens, day to day, after that. I was always aware I was different from other children growing up, not having a mum. I wasn't envious of them, but I missed that female influence and sometimes took out that frustration on my dad.' When Alex was 12, his extreme moods became worse, even though André had decided some years earlier to hire a live-in female tutor in the hope he would benefit from a woman's presence. Nor was the relationship with his father's occasional girlfriends any easier.

"'I was a bit selfish at that age and had grown used to having all his attention,' Alex said. 'It was hard having a woman in the house, as it was a constant reminder you do not have your own mother. Yes, I missed out on not having a mother, but I got plenty of cuddles and affection from my dad.'

"Alex is not close to Rachel's parents – his grandparents, Andrew and Monica Nickell – and has not seen them since he was eight. After Napper's conviction, they spoke of being prevented from seeing their grandson. But Alex insists it has always been his decision not to see them. 'There was a lot of tension between my father and my grandparents, as he felt they were overstepping certain boundaries, while they felt he was being neurotic and overprotective,' he added. 'But I wasn't banned from seeing them. I just found it upsetting being with them. I don't think it's sad. If there are too many conflicts it is better to be apart ... I wrote to them asking for videos they had of my mother. They sent them and said how nice it was to hear from me. Maybe one day we shall meet up again. I don't have anything against them, but they belong to a different world.' What is most striking about Alex is his total lack of bitterness, even in the face of what he considers a lack of professionalism shown by the Metropolitan Police. They failed to stop rapist Napper before he went on to kill his mother, and then took years to link him to her death.

"'My mother would still be alive if the police had done their job properly,' he said. For years, André and Alex were convinced – because the police told them so – that Colin Stagg, a loner who walked his dog on Wimbledon Common, was Rachel's killer. Stagg later received £706,000 in compensation. In contrast Alex received just £90,000 from the Criminal Injuries Compensation Authority. But now, after finding out that his mother's death could have been prevented, he is seeking damages for negligence. A complaint over the Met's alleged failure in its duty of care to Rachel, lodged by Alex and André, is being taken to the European Court of Human Rights.

"'I don't begrudge Colin Stagg a penny – he was wrongly accused and that had to be put right,' Alex said. 'I have little faith in the police. We were told one thing by them, then another, then another.' He added: 'The court action isn't about the money. It's about the police being held to account. I'm not angry, but they haven't done a good job and my mother died as a result.'

"It was in 2003, 11 years after the murder, that a cold case review team using DNA techniques, linked Napper – already convicted for the murders of the Bissets – to DNA samples on Rachel's clothes.

André travelled to the Old Bailey to see him convicted, but Alex chose not to. 'I didn't feel it had anything to offer me,' he said.

"The night before the conviction, André was handed Napper's case history. Shocked by the police's mistakes, he lodged a complaint with the Independent Police Complaints Commission. In June 2010, the IPCC released a damning report concluding the Met had 'missed opportunities' to stop Napper – linked to more than 83 sex attacks – before he killed Rachel.

"So did Alex wonder how his life might have turned out had his mother lived? 'You could play "What if?" all day long if you wanted to,' he said. 'I owe it to myself and my mother to be happy with the life I have.'"

Ripper on the Loose?

1993

A new ripper maniac was being hunted in August 1993 after detectives linked the vicious murders of three sex workers. The man was thought to have strangled the vice girls in the same distinctive way before dumping their naked bodies. He had struck in Norfolk, Bristol and Glasgow. One detective said: "It looks as if we could have a new Yorkshire Ripper-style killer victimising prostitutes." The murderer was believed to be a drifter, lorry driver or travelling salesman. Police feared that he may have claimed more victims. Those known to have died at the time of the investigation were Karen McGregor, Natalie Pearman and Carol Clark. Karen McGregor was found strangled on 19th April 1993 near the Scottish Exhibition and Conference Centre in Clyde, while Natalie, 16, from Mundesley in Norfolk, was found strangled at the Ringland Hills beauty spot three miles from Norwich city centre in November 1992. Police said she worked as a vice girl in Norwich's red-light area. Drug addict Carol Clark, 32, vanished from Bristol on 27th March 1993. Her body was spotted the next day near Sharpness docks in Gloucestershire. Detective Inspector Wayne Murdoch of Gloucestershire police, said: "There are general similarities in all the killings". Other vice girls feared murdered included Mary Duncan, 26, who vanished from Ipswich in July that same year.

The police failed to gain much ground for a number of years, but in March 2000, a man was jailed for life for murdering two sex workers and was suspected of being the serial killer dubbed the Midlands Ripper. Detectives across Britain wanted to interview drifter Alun Kyte about the deaths of other sex workers. Kyte, 35, was given two life sentences after he was found guilty of killing Samo Paull, 20 and 33-year-old Tracey Turner. Single mum Samo's family, who sat through the 11-day trial, cheered when the jury announced their verdict. Mr Justice Crane told Kyte: "You clearly despised these women – but it is also clear that it is you who should be despised." The women's bodies – strangled, half-naked and stripped of jewellery – were found just six miles apart, dumped in country lanes in Leicestershire. But the murders went unsolved until Kyte was caught after a horrific rape three years later. He was jailed for seven years in 1999 for subjecting a woman to a four-hour ordeal at knifepoint when she refused to have sex with him. But then DNA tests matched him to the sperm on Tracey's body. And, while on remand for the rape charge, he confessed to a fellow prisoner: "I killed Tracey", the murder trial in Nottingham was told. Convicted killer Peter Baxter said: "He told me he felt she was laughing at him during a sexual encounter and he couldn't handle it. I remember him saying, 'I just kept strangling her until she stopped laughing.' I gathered he felt some unease in his relationships, particularly with the opposite sex." Three other prisoners also told how Kyte had confessed to the murders. Detectives from as far apart as Lancashire and Gloucester wanted to quiz the murderer about unsolved cases including: Dawn

Shields, 19, in Sheffield, Carol Clark, who suffered massive throat injuries, Janine Downes, found in Telford, Shropshire, and they confirmed they would be looking into the death of Barbara Finn, who had vanished in the red-light district of Hillfields in Coventry. They would also probe the death of mum, Nicola Payne, who disappeared while walking along a shrouded footpath in Willenhall, six weeks later in 1991. Police also wanted to see if there was a connection with the death of Marie Garrity, a sex worker who also vanished from Coventry in 1995. Police had Kyte in their grasp after Tracey was killed, but failed to take a DNA test, it was revealed. David Coleman, Assistant Chief Constable of Leicestershire, said that three weeks after the murder Kyte asked petrol station staff in Birmingham's red-light area about sex workers. Police hunting the killer traced his car through the security video. They found him already serving a jail sentence in Shrewsbury for deception.

Mr Coleman said: "He was interviewed but not DNA swabbed. It is a matter of deep regret that the matter was not resolved then and it is a dent to our personal pride." He also appealed to any woman victim who recognized Kyte's picture to get in touch. He said: "Our task continues. Alun Kyte is an evil, dangerous and wicked man. I do not believe we have uncovered the full extent of his crimes." One detective has always believed that the murders of Samo and Tracey were the work of a serial killer. Detective Superintendent Dave Cox led the original hunt for Tracey's murderer. He firmly believed that Kyte should be pursued.

The US Ripper

1993

A jobless loner who confessed to the murder of at least 20 vice girls led police to two more bodies on Tuesday 29th June 1993. Known as a "mummy's boy", Joel Rifkin, dubbed Joel the Ripper, took officers to the remains hidden in shallow graves. Rifkin picked up £50-a-time sex workers in New York. He said he smothered or strangled most of his victims and stored the bodies in a freezer in his garage before dumping them in remote areas of three states. Like Jack the Ripper, the 34-year-old also butchered the women he preyed on. Police refused to comment on reports that a chainsaw found at his home was used to hack up his victims for burial. Police captain Walter Heesch declared: "We believe him when he says he patronised prostitutes and murdered them." Rifkin, at this stage, looked set to become America's worst serial killer since Jeffrey Dahmer, two years before. Rifkin was arrested as police tried to stop him for driving without number plates. The bespectacled gardener led officers on a wild 20-minute car chase before he was finally stopped. A foul smell drifted from the back of the pick-up truck. "Smells like you've got a body back there," quipped one officer, Sean Ruane. The joking ended when the tied-up corpse of a woman in her twenties was found under a tarpaulin. Rifkin had never had a girlfriend, and he lived with his mother Jean, 71, and sister Jan, 31, on suburban Long Island. He said he used a wheelbarrow to cart bodies to and from the freezer then dumped them in New York State, New Jersey and Connecticut.

In July 1993, it was revealed that pop star Kim Wilde did a photo session with the killer. One of the pictures was found in a scrapbook belonging to the crazed ripper killer, who eventually confessed to murdering 20 sex workers in New York. The keen photographer had conned the British singer into the studio session when she visited the record store where he had worked on Long Island in the early 1980s. She had been in New York as her hit 'Kids In America' was topping the charts. The picture showed Kim Wilde in a pinstriped suit, in the home where he carved up the bodies of his victims. Other pictures showed the pop star posing with some of Rifkin's friends.

His first murder was committed in 1989, when he dismembered the victim and threw her body into the East River. In the following years, he killed another 16 women. Some women were killed in his car, while others were killed at his home. He was also implicated in the murder of a woman whose severed head was found on a New Jersey golf course. It was the head of Heidi Balch, a sex worker, who turned out to be Rifkin's first victim in 1989. His final victim, and the body found in the back of his pick-up, was that of 22-year-old sex worker Tiffany Bresciani. He was found guilty of nine murders in 1994 and sentenced to life in prison of 203 years.

He had begun his long journey to becoming a ripper killer after dreaming of raping and stabbing prostitutes in the early 1970s. By 1989, the violent fantasies could no longer be held back. He picked up a young sex worker called "Susie". With his mother away on business, he was able to take the girl home where he bludgeoned her, hoping to kill her. When that failed, he strangled Susie then dismembered the corpse with an x-acto knife. He removed her identity by severing her fingertips and removing her teeth with pliers. Her arms and torso were tossed into the river in New York, while her head and legs were hidden in Hopewell, New Jersey. Police didn't have a clue about the ripper killer targeting sex workers in New York, and if it wasn't for the fact that his rear number plate was missing as he drove Tiffany's body to his chosen dumping site, they probably wouldn't have caught him for a long while.

David Smith

1999

A "beast" faced a quizzing over 50 sex killings when the brutal sex monster dubbed by police as a modern-day Jack the Ripper was jailed for life on 8th December 1999. David Smith was set to be interviewed about 50 unsolved sex murders across Britain that stretched back 20 years. The 19-stone loner, obsessed with sadomasochistic sex, was convicted at the Old Bailey of killing 22-year-old sex worker Amanda Walker. And, it was revealed that Smith, 43, had struck after being cleared of a horrific carbon copy murder six years earlier because of a legal loophole. He snatched Amanda from a London street, then raped and throttled her, mutilating her body with a knife, before dumping her at a Surrey beauty spot. The Recorder of London, Judge Michael Hyam, told him: "Anyone who has heard what you did to that unfortunate woman after you killed her must have been horrified and revolted. You killed her to satisfy your perverted sexual obsession. You are without pity or remorse." The judge – who was expected to recommend that he be detained for at least 25 years – added: "You are extremely dangerous to women and likely to remain so." At the same court in 1993, lorry driver Smith walked grinning from the dock as he was cleared of murdering sex worker Sarah Crump – butchered with a surgical precision at her bedsit in London. He was freed because the evidence wasn't strong enough. But the jury were not allowed to hear that in the 1970s he served four years in jail for raping a young mum in front of her two young children. When he came out the 6ft 3in man kidnapped a woman and tried to rape her. One detective said: "We believe he is one of the most dangerous sex killers of the century." The reporter from the *Mirror* who saw him walk free was as convinced as all the others that Smith was responsible for Sarah's murder. He was also convinced that the man would kill again, but he just didn't know who until Amanda was viciously and brutally murdered.

In the days after Smith's acquittal, the reporter confronted the murderer at his home. He confronted Smith with the truth, feeling slightly surreal that he was face-to-face with one of Britain's most dangerous killers. Smith denied ever touching Sarah, but he avoided the reporter's gaze. He even admitted to having problems with women in the past. He was a powerful killer, a martial arts expert, cunning and calculating. But unlike the Honey Monster nickname he'd had as a kid, he wasn't a misfit, he was a predatory sex killer, who the reporter had no doubt would rape and murder again. His mum, who believed in his innocence, and probably still does, had most probably made pointless remarks to her son about not approaching women in future, toyed the reporter, who then wrote a story about Smith saying: "Remember this face, it belongs to one of the most violent rapists in Britain." He was undoubtedly a modern Jack the Ripper, freed from court to do as he pleased. He'd had a brilliant QC, Ronnie Thwaites, affable outside court and brutally incisive inside, and Smith walked away from a life sentence. Of course, the jury didn't hear about his previous attacks and the fact that he had spent four years in jail. Another woman kicked out the windows in his minicab in order to escape after he abducted her. He got a two-year suspended sentence. A year later he escaped jail because a sex worker he attacked with a knife was too scared to give evidence. Just 17 days before Sarah died he was acquitted of trying to murder a sex worker. The jury had also been spared seeing photos of Sarah's body. She had been disembowelled and had her breasts cut off. Detective Inspector Jill McTigue, who led the investigation into Smith, knew it was only a matter of time before he struck again. He wasn't a normal human being and did indeed have the potential to be a serial killer. Following his acquittal, Smith wasted little time immersing himself in his favourite pastimes – prostitution and sadomasochistic sex. He led a double life, working as a lorry driver near Heathrow and spending nights running his own escort agency. Smith's lust for murder returned on 24th April.

He went to a fetish party complete with dungeon in Ilford, Essex, where he paid £110 and spent an hour in the steam room with a redhead. There was no sexual contact even though they were almost naked. Smith scared the woman by saying he could kill in seconds. He hurt her by gripping her hand and then boasted that he did not feel pain himself. When he left he drove off to find a prostitute. That person was Amanda Walker, a six-stone mum from Leeds with a two-year-old son. Her fate was sealed when Smith picked her up near Paddington station. He bound her hands, repeatedly raped her and mutilated her body before burying it at Wisley in Surrey. Amanda had managed to split Smith's lip and his blood had dripped onto her bra. Smith was arrested when police found her clothes smeared with his blood less than a mile from his home. They also found his fingerprint on her handbag. He also admitted to killing Amanda to another prisoner while on remand.

In December 1999, the *Mirror* reported: "The scars are still there. Some you can see, like the five knife wounds beneath her breast. Others are hidden, the mental scars of discovering that the man she had married was an evil sex fiend suspected by police of raping and murdering as many as 50 women." Michelle Thomas read with mounting horror the catalogue of her former husband's suspected crimes and wondered how on earth she had survived. She spoke for the first time after his conviction for the murder of Amanda. She still trembled with terror at the thought she could have become a victim who was raped, throttled and mutilated like so many others. After years of silence, Michelle spoke exclusively to the *Mirror* of her nightmare marriage to Smith. He had tried to kill her three times, and she revealed how when she finally fled from him, Smith warned her: "I'll find you wherever you are". Twenty years before, Smith had been a sad, impotent man, unable even to consummate his own marriage. He never made love to his wife in more than two years, his only thrills came from playing deadly knife games – slashing her below her breasts in play-jousting, with a lethal blade. "David had a problem with sex," said Michelle who divorced him in the early 1980s. He was depressed and frustrated, so he read pornographic magazines and started taking his wife's knickers to work. She was never advised that the man she had married had been to jail for rape.

Things escalated and one morning, after Smith lit a candle and left for work, Michelle and two of her young daughters from a previous relationship woke up to a flat filled with smoke. The fire brigade had to kick in the door and drag them out. The family were rehoused and things settled, but one Sunday afternoon, after a minor row, Smith drove his car into the middle of the road – straight into the path of an oncoming vehicle. Michelle, clutching her youngest daughter, was thrown through the windscreen. Not long after, Smith's fetish for knives grew more dangerous and he was forever shouting and throwing tantrums. He always carried a knife with him, and he used to joust with them, and the playing got out of hand. But the nightmare got worse and one evening she discovered Smith and others sitting around a table that was "covered in drugs". She tried to leave the room, but Smith threw her back in. He injected her with heroin until she passed out. She woke up a week later in intensive care. A terrified Michelle went on the run. Smith continued to try to track her down. Then police arrived at her door wanting to make sure she was still alive after the attack on Sarah. Six weeks after they found the body of Amanda, the police traced Michelle and again knocked on her front door. She'd given them a statement for the Sarah case, and this time they wanted her to be a witness. In the end she wasn't on the witness list and she was overwhelmed with relief when he was convicted. Michelle had also been through a terrible ordeal at the hands of Smith, but because she had married him, she was also sick inside and said: "I knew him. I married him. What does that make me?"

The Camden Ripper

2003

Detectives hunting the bodies in bags murderer in January 2003 named their prime suspect as Anthony John Hardy – a schizophrenic recluse – and made a grim warning that he should not be approached. Scotland Yard launched a nationwide search for Hardy, a man in his fifties, after body parts were found at his flat. Detective Chief Superintendent David Cook said: "He should be treated with extreme caution and is clearly dangerous. Anyone who knows where he is should contact police." The manhunt followed the horrific discovery of a torso and legs of a woman and girl dumped in bin bags in Camden, North London. When police searched Hardy's nearby home they found a second torso sealed in a bin liner. A hacksaw, believed to have been used to dismember the bodies, was lying nearby. The walls of the dingy flat were daubed with pagan-style symbols, including a large black cross. Half the ceiling was painted red with yellow patterns, and a black stiletto shoe lay on a windowsill. In a bizarre twist, police revealed that the body of a prostitute was found at the flat a year before – but an investigation concluded she had died of natural causes. Hardy, an outpatient at a local psychiatric unit, was described by neighbours as "scary". A day later, the police announced that they wanted to interview Hardy over 12 more ripper-style killings.

Amazingly, the fugitive spent four hours unnoticed in a hospital shortly after his photo was released by Scotland Yard and was even caught on CCTV. Detectives were also desperate to trace Kelly Ann Nicol, 25, who had not been seen since she was spotted with Hardy near his home on Boxing Day. It was now 3rd January. Commander Andrew Baker, head of Scotland Yard's Homicide Squad, said: "We are extremely worried about her safety and need to find her very quickly. She may be in danger." The other murders that police needed to quiz Hardy over included that of Paula Fields, a 31-year-old sex worker from Liverpool whose dismembered remains were found in six carrier bags dumped in a canal near the killer's flat in 2001. Her body had been sawn up with a hacksaw. Two months earlier, the dismembered body of Zoe Parker, 25, a London prostitute, was found in the Thames. When Hardy had walked into the hospital he had given his correct name and said he wanted some pills for his diabetic condition. He walked out four hours later without the medication. He had changed his appearance. He had shaved off his beard and appeared to have cut his hair. Kelly had tattoos so the police knew that the two lots of female remains they found at Hardy's flat were not her, but there was still no trace of the young woman. The body parts had been found by a homeless man looking for food in dustbins in the Camden area. It was believed that the two women were both sex workers.

It was then revealed in the press that Hardy had been released from a psychiatric hospital in 2002 after doctors said he posed no threat to the public. He had been detained after prostitute Rose White had been found dead in his home. It was thought that the 38-year-old had died of natural causes, but now police weren't so sure. By 4th January 2003 Hardy had been in police custody for 24 hours and was questioned by police about the dismembered remains of the two women found in and around his flat. Hardy had attended university in London where he qualified as a mechanical engineer. He had married and fathered four children. The whole family emigrated to Tasmania in the 1980s, but when the Hardys' marriage collapsed in the early 1990s, he returned to Britain. He became an alcoholic who struggled to find work. By the time Hardy was arrested over the two women in 2003, both the victims' hands and heads were still missing.

Hardy appeared in court on 6th January 2003 charged with murdering three women. They included Rose White and the two dismembered women found in Camden, where one was named as Elizabeth Valad, a 29-year-old sex worker from Nottingham, who was identified by the serial numbers on the implants in her breasts and buttocks. Kelly Nichol was, however, traced in Camden and found to be alive and well. She had encountered Hardy but thought he was odd. She was convinced that Hardy thought she was a sex worker – in reality she was homeless – and she refused to go off with him. By 7th January his third victim was named as New Zealand-born Brigitte Cathy MacClennan. Her distraught family only heard the news when it was announced on TV.

Forensic evidence showed traces of blood "virtually all over the flat" and pornographic photos of the dead women were found. Tony Hardy was jailed for life in November 2003 after pleading guilty to three murders.

Ripper Killers in the 21st Century

In 2004, a man who battered a gay lecturer to death then hacked up his body was jailed for life. Robert McMahon, 24, smashed Mark Green's skull with a gas canister, cut off his legs and head and then asked his brother James at knifepoint to help bury him. He was buried in the garden of James' Coventry home. He received two years for aiding his brother in his grisly crime. Then, in 2008, evil Derek Brown was quizzed over fears that he butchered dozens more women after he was found guilty of murdering two women and police believed they had been butchered. He claimed he wanted to be like Jack the Ripper. Xiao Mel Go and Bonnie Barrett suffered agonizing deaths at the hands of Brown. He picked up the victims – both mums – in London's Whitechapel and convinced himself he would gain notoriety as a serial ripper killer. The Old Bailey heard how Brown targeted vulnerable women who he thought would not be missed. Their bodies have never been found, but police believed they were mutilated as Brown bought a saw, knife, rubber gloves and plastic sacks before the killings. They were confident that he had cut up their bodies and disposed of them using an industrial compactor. Their bloodstains were found on the doors, walls and ceiling. Brown was obsessed with ripper killers.

In 2009, Korena Roberts was charged with murder after police found the body of a missing 21-year-old in a cupboard in her flat.

Pregnant Heather Snively had been cut open at the stomach so her unborn child could be removed, a post-mortem revealed. She had also been beaten around the head with several weapons. Roberts had called an ambulance when the baby became ill. Paramedics were unable to revive the child and called police after they realized she was not the mother. However, she had been claiming for months that she was pregnant and told her boyfriend and friends she was expecting twins. She met the victim, who lived nearby, on an internet site, and the two women had planned to swap baby clothes. If the baby was alive when removed from the tragic mother's womb, Roberts would face a second murder charge. It was not the first case of its kind in the US. Andrea Curry-Demus, 38, was awaiting trial after pregnant 18-year-old Kia Johnson was tied up, drugged and had her uterus sliced open. The baby survived. In 2007, Lisa Montgomery, 39, was given the death sentence for killing 23-year-old Bobbi Jo Stinnett and stealing her unborn baby.

The Long Island Ripper

2010

A terrified young woman hared down the dark street screaming: "They're trying to kill me." Before a startled passer-by could react, the girl vanished. This incident constitutes the last known movements of 24-year-old sex worker Shannan Gilbert. Detectives investigating her mysterious disappearance from Long Island, New York, in May 2010, had no luck at that time finding out what happened to the young woman, but along a deserted highway, they stumbled upon eight other dead bodies, most of them sex workers. Shortly after, two more sets of human remains were found. Detectives linked the murders with those of four prostitutes who were found dead in nearby Atlantic City. Investigators believed all the killings were the work of one man who was dubbed the Long Island Ripper. In an extraordinary twist, they also believed that he was a policeman.

One officer said: "He is a guy aware of how we utilise technology. Frankly, people are thinking he may be a cop – either one still in law enforcement or one who has moved on. Without question, this guy is smart, this guy is not a dope. It's a guy who thinks about things." The murders sent shockwaves through Long Island – a millionaires' playground. It was the worst serial-killing spree to hit New York since the "Son of Sam", David Berkowitz, shot six people dead in the 1970s. Police had so far found the remains of seven adults, one toddler and a bundle of bones thought to belong to two people – taking the body count to 10. There could have been more – and there were a string of theories about the killer's identity. Investigators argued that differences in the way the victims were killed, the disposal of the bodies, DNA evidence and Shannan's last cries could even point to more than one murderer. All the sex workers found murdered had placed advertisements on Craigslist. Four sex workers were found along Ocean Parkway by officers searching for Shannan. Each of the bodies had been wrapped in a sack-like cloth and were found clustered within 500 feet of each other. Police had to expand their massive search for the killer from Long Island's Suffolk County westward into the Jones Beach area of Nassau County, over the border from New York City. By 2011 police confirmed that they were looking for two men in connection with the murders and that they believed both men could be police officers. However, it was eventually concluded that the murders were the work of one man and that Shannan Gilbert was not one of his victims. To this day, the Long Island Ripper's identity is unknown. He is still out there ...